EVERTON
100 SEASONS AT THE TOP

GWLADYS STREET'S

BLUE
BOOK

David France + David Prentice

600 SUBSCRIBERS

1 Everton Football Club	2 Hilary Watson	3 Elizabeth France	4 Melanie Prentice
5 Rochelle Labone	6 Nora Mercer	7 Nancy Young	8 Lesley Ball
9 Barbara Dean	10 Janet Royle	11 Pat Hickson	12 Clare Gray
13 Philip Carter	14 Bill Kenwright	15 Arthur Abercromby	16 Paul Gregg
17 Keith Tamlin	18 Jon Woods	19 Michael Dunford	20 David Moyes
21 Peter King	22 David Uren	23 Martin O'Boyle	24 Barry Hewitt
25 Len Capeling	26 Garry Doolan	27 Chris Gill	28 Vic Gibson
29 Mike Hughes	30 Ian MacDonald	31 Steven Milne	32 Mark O'Brien
33 George Orr	34 Mark Staniford	35 Mark Tallentire	36 Noel Gornell
37 Seth Batterby	38 Paul Watts	39 Phil Caton	40 Peter L Parry
41 Jack Pate	42 Stephen Drake	43 John Sinnott	44 Henry Lightfoot
45 Paul Ashcroft	46 Paul Banks	47 Andrew Conway	48 John Ribchester
49 Andrew Jones	50 Brian Tottey	51 Liam Mulcahy	52 J Alistair Davies
53 Andy Hunter	54 Ben Everson	55 Gary Hegarty	56 Karl A Gates
57 Jimmy Mulville	58 Philip Orme	59 Andy Clarke	60 K P Jones
61 Dave Davies	62 Ian Brownlow	63 Richard Coultas	64 Dennis Hayes
65 Steve Vick	66 Keith Wilson	67 Charles Simpson	68 Clifton Vaughan
69 George Bordessa	70 Ron Coomber	71 Sid Hooper	72 Charles Morton
73 David Podmore	74 Peter Ludley	75 Glyn Minshall	76 Frederick Paul Kennerley
77 Graeme Harkness	78 Richard Humphrey	79 Christopher Woods	80 John W Brotheridge
81 Mark Grogan	82 Colin Jenkins	83 Tony Hambidge	84 Paul R Simpson
85 Robert Herbert	86 Stephen Maloney	87 Richard Dowthwaite	88 Christopher A Simpson
89 Robin Peters	90 Phil Heron	91 Bill Mounty	92 Matthew R Simpson
93 Michael York	94 Richard Spencer	95 Matthew Holt	96 James P McCartney
97 Percy Harwood	98 Lilian Cobon	99 Matt Noon	100 Heather Woltz
101 Paul McIver	102 Barry Harrison	103 Dave Sheen	104 John T Pickersgill
105 Mike Saunders	106 Colin Lord	107 Norman Jones	108 Finn Willy Fosen
109 Chris Marsh	110 Allan Bennett	111 Dave Youds	112 Tony Gavin
113 Ethan Bloor	114 Stuart Simpson	115 Fred Warburton	116 David Starsky
117 Harry Powell	118 Christopher Barber	119 Martin Ellis	120 Chris Byrne
121 William Pritchard	122 Lawrence Cuddy	123 John Kobiela	124 John Derek Holden
125 Noel Harbage	126 David Storey	127 Barry Connell	128 Michael Connell
129 Liam Pidgeon	130 Andrew Skinner	131 Dave Tafner	132 Frank Fitzsimmons
133 Steve Mahon	134 Eddie Major	135 James Philpott	136 Peter Gordon Winstanley
137 Jon Beck	138 Brian Lawley	139 Billy Flanagan	140 Dennis Stevens
141 Anthony Polak	142 Ian Pilkington	143 John Blain	144 Geoffrey Ormesher
145 Adrian Jackson	146 John Thompson	147 Steven Taylor	148 Martin Boulton

149 Phil Parker	150 George Wood	151 Malcolm Menard	152 Ron Jones
153 Jim Barrow	154 Neil Parkinson	155 Graham Wood	156 Gary A Donnelly
157 Ralph Carson	158 Michael Singer	159 Ian Andrews	160 Benjamin Wood
161 Bernard Sharkey	162 Peter Byrne	163 Donald Ferns	164 Martin Bartholomew
165 Jack Chauveau	166 William Williams	167 Jamie Davies	168 Ian Bartholomew
169 Jon Hirshman	170 Steven Hilton	171 Andrew Hilton	172 John Heyes
173 Andrew Colson	174 John Allman	175 Karen Burke	176 Ronald G Rimmer
177 Joseph Boden	178 Gerard Boden	179 Paul Heyes	180 Brian Ferguson
181 Tony Birtles	182 Ian Burrows	183 Debbie Lloyd	184 Alyce Molly Heeley
185 Brian Doran	186 David Doran	187 John Doran	188 Thomas Doran
189 Keith Asquith	190 Brian Coghlan	191 Neville Powell	192 Gordon MacKenzie
193 Mark Allen	194 Robert Butler	195 Man-Cho Choi	196 Karla Boulton
197 Tony Fletcher	198 Stan Fletcher	199 Brian Roche	200 Elizabeth McClarnon
201 Paul Dwyer	202 Richard Gallie	203 Eddie Cross	204 Michael Cross
205 Marian Rothwell	206 Norman Owens	207 Paul Williams	208 John Paul Dykhuizen
209 Carl Hopwood	210 Terence Nelson	211 Dave Vivyan	212 Arthur R Mullett
213 Keith Grace	214 Ted Brookes	215 Steve Murphy	216 Darren Hoare
217 John Collins	218 David Maples	219 Lee Harrison	220 Callum Williams
221 Ann Edey	222 Tony Dove	223 Alan Simpson	224 Robert James Lowe
225 Alan Dalc	226 Colin Massey	227 Jimmy Walker	228 Mark Chester
229 Tommy Price	230 Vivienne Brimilow	231 William Pike	232 W T Roberts
233 Oliver Williams	234 Steve Leonard	235 Paddy Hayes	236 Graham Hugh Atkinson
237 Calum Beardwood	238 Eric Moonman	239 Josh Moonman	240 H Arwel Hughes
241 John Thornberry	242 Matthew Gye	243 Colette Bennett	244 Manda Bennett
245 Barry Spencer	246 Harry Trybshaw	247 Alexander Walker	248 Ian Sherbrooke
249 Paula Wilkinson	250 Paul Fletcher	251 Graham Williams	252 David T Sheppard
253 Chris Sexton	254 Tom Sanders	255 Stephen Dunford	256 George W Burgess
257 Frank McCann	258 Colin White	259 Francis Baccino	260 Ronald F Tennant
261 Harold Aaron	262 Peter Lindop	263 John Norman	264 Gary Pepper
265 Keith Maddocks	266 Vic Morton	267 Dave Worbey	268 Dave Bennett
269 Nik Allen	270 David Southern	271 Timothy O'Malley	272 David Jones
273 Julie Wood	274 Terry Wood	275 David Bates	276 Brian Johnson
277 John Fowler	278 Paul Fowler	279 Joseph O'Keefe	280 Victor Peers
281 Mike Downey	282 Donal Morgan	283 David Sharp	284 Carol Davies
285 Thomas Homer	286 Dave Cartwright	287 David Jones	288 Howard Parr
289 Francis Furlong	290 Michael Furlong	291 Jim Crilly	292 Peter Delaney
293 Paul McNamara	294 Geoff Cadman	295 Steve Jones	296 Linda Hayward
297 James Gielty	298 Kevin Parr	299 Jim Cooper	300 Phil Redmond

301 Lucy Hackett	302 Joanne Hackett	303 Peter Hackett	304 Emma Tyson
305 Kathy Beechouk	306 Robert Ward	307 Ken Gane	308 John A Ferguson
309 Mark Gallagher	310 Norman Swindells	311 David Swainston	312 William Audley
313 Lew Connor	314 Graham Bethell	315 Mark Bethell	316 Tony McDonald
317 Thomas Lupton	318 Keith Gilchrist	319 Dennis Gourley	320 Michael Doyle
321 Gerard Crighton	322 Max Polmear	323 Michael Lamont	324 David J S Owens
325 Paul Kelly	326 Martin Beesley	327 Chris Cain	328 Nigel French
329 Kevin Conway	330 Trevor Kenney	331 Denise Lyons	332 Gerard Lyons
333 Neville Smith	334 Paul Silsby	335 Neil Cox	336 Harry Mousley
337 Phil Homer	338 Anthony Corns	339 Ron Redfern	340 Andrew Gleeson
341 Frank Christian	342 Stephen Percival	343 Steven Mitchell	344 Bill Grundy
345 Keith Abbott	346 Geoff Nash	347 Karl Nash	348 Raymond Forward
349 Lee Evans	350 Dave Whiteside	351 Phil Pellow	352 John R Rowlands
353 Kevin Morrissey	354 Simon Coyle	355 William Adams	356 John R Beamish
357 William Kearney	358 Keith Dickinson	359 Brian Tweedle	360 Shaneela Vohra
361 William Mair	362 John Booth	363 Kenneth Booth	364 Stephen Prandle
365 Gareth Barkley	366 Ray Hughes	367 Trevor Dickson	368 Carl Vanderwerff
369 Nick Chamberlain	370 Paul Bennett	371 Bob Johnson	372 Brian B Paulson
373 Neil Jones	374 Trevor Skempton	375 Michael Wood	376 James Prendergast
377 Chris Dow	378 Bill Hornby	379 Tony Condron	380 Christopher Powell
381 Scott Wall	382 Paul Stanley	383 Evertony Shortall	384 Jonathan Robertson
385 Jonathan Addy	386 David Howman	387 Colin Prescott	388 Oliver Dalton
389 Nigel Sartain	390 Steve Jones	391 Peter Young	392 James John Conway
393 Darren Cook	394 Jack Clarke	395 Jack Cunningham	396 Howard Cunningham
397 Christian Keegan	398 Frank Keegan	399 Roger McGough	400 Roger Long
401 Peter Kaiser	402 Steve Kaiser	403 Robert Robinson	404 Brian Birchall
405 Ian Webb	406 Colin Hincks	407 Robert Edmunds	408 Cavan Cannon
409 Ian Turnbull	410 Christopher Jones	411 Ben Johnson	412 Philip Crilly
413 Richard Whittall	414 Simon Evans	415 Lee Ellis	416 Alex Phillips
417 Stephen Hickson	418 Rod Cullinone	419 Sarah Jordan	420 Mark Jordan
421 Jerry Burns	422 Dave Moore	423 Tony Moore	424 David Howard
425 Leo Forsey	426 Edward Bartley	427 Neil Lewis	428 Phil Mann
429 Tommy Connor	430 Stan Brierley	431 Vic Wright	432 Andrew Steven Haller
433 Eddie Holmes	434 Vic Poole	435 Mike Wilson	436 Andrew Edwards
437 Keith Richmond	438 Ian Murray	439 George Hoffman	440 Sean McAdam
441 Rosa Harrison	442 Nicholas Marsh	443 Ian Buffey	444 Brian Snagg
445 Jim Callinan	446 Ruaraidh Callinan	447 Stanley McQuillan	448 A W Daddy

449 Dave Kelly	450 Billy Butler	451 Billy McClure	452 Steve Owens
453 Adrian McGrath	454 Martin Thwaite	455 Joe Baker	456 Mark Gawne
457 John Livingstone	458 Adam Shepphard	459 Brian Harney	460 Karl Masters
461 Aaron Hawkins	462 Antony Hawkins	463 Tommy Murray	464 John Thompson
465 Holly Chance	466 Neil Chance	467 Kevin Quinn	468 Gillian Sutherland
469 Andy Edwards	470 Matty Edwards	471 Phil Edwards	472 Adam Jones
473 Chris Newton	474 Ian Newton	475 Robert Armstrong	476 James McKiernan
477 Don Maclure	478 Wilfred Smith	479 Barry Steele	480 Ted Carless
481 Andrew Connor	482 Christopher Connor	483 Kyle McEllin	484 Lindsay Millington
485 Donald Birchall	486 Ben Collier	487 Gordon Doran	488 John Huddleston Jones
489 Frank Malone	490 John Croft	491 Stephen Mahoney	492 Paul Williams
493 Ray Cunliffe	494 Stan Hughes	495 Stephen Samuels	496 Andy W Costain
497 Brendan Connolly	498 Daniel Connolly	499 Andy McCormick	500 John Dwyer

501 Darren Griffiths	502 Mark Rowan	503 Ian Kidd	504 Robert James Perraton
505 Kenneth Kelly	506 Andrew Roberts	507 Clive Bailey	508 P J Hunter
509 Maria Hanlon	510 Michael Hanlon	511 John Raftery	512 Christopher Beesley
513 Mark Fyfield	514 Dale Tomaselli	515 Kevin Hardman	516 John Huddleston McGovern
517 Roy Coulson	518 Joan O'Donovan	519 David Shepherd	520 William Adams
521 Jimmy Connor	522 Bill Jones	523 Kieran Buckley	524 Claire Louise Jones
525 Michael Hughes	526 Harry Ellison	527 James Egan	528 Kenneth Jones
529 Gordon Jones	530 Stephen Draper	531 Kevin Rogers	532 Michael Shearon Weller
533 Tom Cawley	534 Phil Jones	535 Frank Thwaite	536 Tim Shearon Johnson
537 Mark Parker	538 Brian Jones	539 Russell Crerar	540 Ben O'Donnell
541 John Oxton	542 Peter McGrath	543 Michael Driscoll	544 George Woodhouse
545 David Thompson	546 Edna Thompson	547 Stuart Robbins	548 Deborah J Daniels
549 Ian Foulkes	550 Dave Atherton	551 David Rooney	552 Gareth M Davies
553 Paul Cunniff	554 Ron Parker	555 Sean McQueen	556 Christopher Cooper
557 Michael McCann	558 Gordon Doran	559 Bernard Williams	560 John Reddington
561 Ben Cox	562 Eleanor Cox	563 Josh Cox	564 Philip William Roberts
565 Melanie Lewis	566 John O'Boyle	567 Frank Malone	568 Charles McDonald
569 Mike Royden	570 Sylvia Hallwood	571 Anton Cook	572 Iain Green
573 Graham Temple	574 John Nicholas	575 Derek Richardson	576 Margaret Yeardsley
577 Ann Bedford	578 Ian Critchley	579 Dave Williams	580 Steve Dingsdale
581 Michael McKeown	582 Eddie Hourston	583 Lee Challinor	584 Shane Challinor
585 Ray Wynne	586 Keith Jones	587 Jessica Jones	588 Ronnie Williams
589 David Jackson	590 Jack Lambert	591 Jonathan Canty	592 Neil Turton
593 Alan Rice	594 George Tudor	595 Miles Tudor	596 Glyn Tudor
597 Agnes Ireland	598 Brian Alexander	599 Becky Tallentire	600 L Norman Cohen

This book is dedicated to the memory of

Gordon Watson
(1914-2001)

Every Evertonian should be fiercely proud that we are the first club to celebrate the unique achievement of a century of seasons in top flight football. I know that Gordon Watson, who was employed by the club in one way or another for the majority of them, certainly was. And it is wholly appropriate that he was given the opportunity to share his recollections from his many roles at Goodison Park with a wider audience.

Gordon, who passed away while this book was in the process of publication, spent the best years of his life offering unstinting service to Everton. As a player, he was admired as one of the finest passers of the ball in the pre-war game, a period when he displayed his skills alongside Tommy Lawton, TG Jones and Joe Mercer in the 1938/39 title-winning side.

After hanging up his boots, he joined the backroom staff and helped to develop a legion of stars including Brian Labone, Colin Harvey and Joe Royle. He later transferred to the promotions department and also served the club as barman, steward and stadium tour guide. When Gordon finally retired from active duties in 1997, aged 83, he maintained his lifelong love of the Blues by watching them from the stands.

This book, based on his candid day-to-day observations, is a lasting legacy.

Forewords

Everton Football Club is second to none ... it will always be my club, just as it always remained Gordon Watson's club.

I served eight all too short years as a player, then another regrettably curtailed spell as manager of our cherished football club. Despite a recent close shave, following Wayne Rooney's meteoric rise into first-team football, I am still the youngest League debutant in our illustrious history. It is that achievement which I am probably proudest of, when you think of the hundreds upon hundreds of footballers who have been honoured to pull on the royal blue of Everton. But there again, I was gratified to be reminded that not only was the 1995 FA Cup the last trophy to land at Goodison, it was the last time an English manager had captured any major silverware. Further success is long overdue but that should not detract from our achievement of 100 campaigns in the top flight of football. That is eight more than any other member of football's aristocracy and testimony to our outstanding levels of consistency and ambition.

Of course, I am immensely proud of my part in the history of Everton but cannot claim anything like the level of service that Gordon Watson achieved. He worked with and watched the vast majority of the players featured in this book - and was there at the start of my career, too. In fact, he was the man who conveyed the message to me on the Friday morning before the first-team trip to Blackpool in January 1966 that Harry Catterick wanted to see me upstairs in his office. The news that the manager gave me was that I would be making my debut the following day.

That isn't my earliest recollection of Gordon Watson, though. He was a coach when I first started training at Bellefield and I can still recall what an excellent striker of a ball he was, even then when he must have been in his fifties. It was evident to everyone that Gordon had been a footballer of some quality. He loved to practice passing with the younger players and while we tried to work on our own techniques, we would watch him with immense admiration as he pinged the ball effortlessly around the Bellefield gym. Of course, that role was just one of five or six he filled during a life devoted to Everton. He was blue through and through and never grumbled when he was asked to do something different.

Gordon was a lovely, lovely man and I was delighted when I heard that he had committed his thoughts to paper before his death. He certainly had plenty of tales to share and must have had the authors in stitches. Both authors are devoted Evertonians - just like me. I've attended the Hall of Fame Galas organised by David France - and while the following days have always been a struggle, the nights themselves have been electric! When I was manager of Everton I enjoyed working closely with David Prentice in his role at the *Liverpool Echo* - I speak regularly with him and still trust him. Both Davids are ideally qualified to transfer Gordon's insights into the printed word and I hope that you enjoy reading them as much as he, no doubt, enjoyed telling them.

Always remember ... once a Blue, always a Blue.

Foreword by Joe Royle

Everton's contribution to the beautiful game is immeasurable. Even after I've taken off my blue-tinted glasses and rubbed my eyes, I see that no other English club comes close. Therefore as followers of the royal blue persuasion commemorate our 100 seasons in the top flight of the game, I find it most fitting that we salute the men who have worn our famous colours with such distinction since the pioneering days at St Domingo chapel. This book provides a unique insight into some 200 plus men who have left their mark in one way or another and I feel privileged to be associated with it.

I'm often asked how the players of bygone eras would shape up against their modern counterparts. It's a tough one to answer, given our natural penchant for endowing our favourites from the past with golden auras and the occasional halo. It seems that the few individuals that we care to remember often become immortalised as even greater players with the passing of time. However, I expect that this book will make things much clearer. Why? Because it's based on the consistent judgements of a well-qualified Blue who either saw these men up-close or knew an equally respected Blue who had. The decision to document the personal opinions of Gordon Watson, who spent going on seven decades at Goodison, was a stroke of genius and ensures that future generations have a more accurate yardstick to debate the deeds and contributions of players from different periods in the club's history.

Perhaps more than anything, the integrity of this publication is reflected in the devotion of those involved in its production. When I learned that these three Blues were putting their heads together, I knew that they would come up with something special. Silver-tongued Gordon loved to talk football and the two authors have that rare ability to listen. I owe Gordon a huge debt because he taught me how to master the ball. He was highly regarded by everyone and it was obvious that he knew a lot about the game and the men who played it. While I never forgave him for being Harry Catterick's time-keeper at Bellefield, or for the resulting fines for being late for training, I had the upmost respect for him as a coach and as someone who had played with Dean, Mercer and Lawton. Likewise I owe a huge debt to David France and David Prentice. The former's devotion has been demonstrated by his establishment of Gwladys Street's Hall of Fame, which puts the Nuremburg Rally and the Oscars to shame, and Blueblood which is dedicated to alleviating the medical hardships of our old boys. His efforts have resulted in dozens of pain-free lives and much more. The latter has been employed in a lifetime's labour of love chronicling the activities at Everton. I look forward to his daily deliverances but will never forgive him for marrying Bill Dean's grand-daughter. Melanie was the apple of Dixie's eye - and mine too!

Like Messrs Watson, France and Prentice, I love Everton. So much so that these days my personal mission is to spread the good word about 'The People's Club' wherever and whenever I can. Believe it or not, there are still some unbelievers out there! Clearly, this book will make my task much easier. It is great to reminisce about the heroes featured in this tremendous tome but, while we look back with immense pride, it is paramount that a progressive club should also live in the present and prepare for the future.

Never forget ... one Blue is worth twenty Reds.

Brian Labone

THE AUTHORS ...

David France is a management consultant based in Houston, Texas. He specialises in the re-structuring of under-performing companies world-wide. Dr France was the founder of The Everton Former-Players' Foundation, aka Blueblood.

His other Everton books include:
Toffee Cards - The Tobacco Years (ISBN 1-874799-05-9)
Toffee Pages - The Post-War Years (ISBN 1-874799-06-7)
Gwladys Street's Hall of Fame (ISBN 1-874799-09-1)
Gwladys Street's Hall of Fame - Edition II (ISBN 1-874799-10-5)
Gwladys Street's Hall of Fame - Edition III (ISBN 1-874799-12-1)
Gwladys Street's Holy Trinity - Kendall, Harvey & Ball (ISBN 1-874799-14-8)
Gwladys Street's Big Book for kids of all ages (ISBN 1-874799-15-6)

David Prentice has been the Everton correspondent of the *Liverpool Echo* since 1993, during which time he has interviewed seven Everton managers and a plethora of boys in blue. He has even taken his work home with him, marrying 'Dixie' Dean's grand-daughter whom he met at the first Gwlady's Street Hall of Fame Gala. Mr Prentice is also a trustee of Blueblood.

ACKNOWLEDGMENTS ...

Many Evertonians have committed their time and energy to produce this book. In particular the authors would like to thank Elizabeth France, Melanie Prentice and Hilary Watson for their patience and encouragement.

They would like to express their sincere appreciation to John Bailey, Sandy Brown, Len Capeling, Garry Doolan, John Dwyer, Bill Edgar, Wally Fielding, Vic Gibson, Chris Gill, Brian Harris, Dave Hickson, Mike Hughes, Jimmy Husband, Tommy Jones, Bill Kenwright, Brian Labone, Ian MacDonald, Steven Milne, Martin O'Boyle, Mark O'Brien, Jimmy O'Neill, George Orr, Fred Pickering, Ian Ross, Joe Royle, Becky Tallentire, Mark Tallentire, Gordon West, Alan Whittle, Richard Whitehead and Keith Wilson for their help.

The authors are indebted to Barry Hewitt for validating the statistical data and to Alan Hodgkins, Peter King and Dave Uren, three football fans of a different persuasion, and Nick Cook for their creative inputs.

GWLADYS STREET'S BLUE BOOK CONTENTS ...

Five minutes everybody ... Break a leg!

Singing The Blues

This is my first book and my last. It took one year to help write and more than sixty to research. I think of it as my bequest to my royal blue family who radiate a collective warmth that puts more conventional families to shame.

Everton Football Club has been my life. I was conscripted as a teenager and in all honesty didn't have much say in the matter. I remember playing on a miserable Saturday afternoon for Blyth Spartans against Sunderland Reserves when at half-time my father took me to one side and informed me that I'd been transferred to the Toffees. A few days later, as my train chugged towards Lime Street I had to pinch myself - it was a dream come true. I had joined one of the most famous football clubs in the world and was about to rub shoulders with Warney Cresswell, Ted Sagar and the legendary William Ralph Dean.

I worked really hard at improving my passing game and my proudest accomplishment in those early years was our Central League championship triumph. With an angry Bill Dean leading the attack, while at odds with the club's powerbrokers, it was hardly surprising that we carried off the trophy with ease. Eventually, I managed to fight my way into the first-team where I seemed to flourish alongside the likes of TG Jones, Tommy Lawton and Joe Mercer. We were all so very young and so naive but our School of Science brand of football won the League championship and also captured the imagination of fans nationwide. To be honest, we thought that we were destined for a decade of greatness but, after just three games, the new season was cancelled and all of the lads were conscripted into the forces or defence-related occupations. I worked at Harland & Wolff throughout World War II along with Torry Gillick and Wally Boyes and was able to turn out for Everton in regional football. It seems to me that Everton and war-time sacrifices go hand-in-hand. Shortly after the club had won the 1915 championship, the Great War erupted. And shortly after the 1985 title success, the Heysel hostilities undermined our ambitions.

I played a few post-war seasons and took my tally to over 250 first-team appearances for my one and only club before hanging up my boots. Subsequently I took up coaching and adored working with the wealth of young talent on the Goodison books. Of course by the early sixties, Mr Moores' cheque book had also attracted several household names and we were hailed as 'The Merseyside Millionaires'. That's not to say that the club's benefactor threw his money around like confetti. Far from it! In particular I recall that during the American Soccer Cup tournament, Everton trained in New York's Central Park. We changed in a park shelter which was supervised by a wise-cracking Yank called Hank. He looked after our kit, ran errands and generally helped to make the lads feel at home. Nothing was too much trouble for him so at the end of our stay I tipped him $10 in appreciation for his services. However Mr Moores disapproved and instructed me to recover the gratuity. Embarrassingly I explained my dilemma to Hank. His wrinkled black face grinned at me through his cloud of cigar smoke. A few minutes later he approached both Mr Moores and Mr Holland-Hughes, the club chairman, clutching a rusty container labelled 'Tips' and emptied the contents of nickels and dimes at the feet of the Littlewoods Pools billionaire. Training came to a standstill as all of New York city watched Mr Moores kneel down in the grass and count the pieces of silver.

Americans say that if you find a job that you enjoy then you will never have to work a day in your life. Well I was at Everton for 64 years and loved every minute. The time simply flew by. I have so many fond memories and feel privileged to have enjoyed day-to-day interactions with some great characters. Who were the best?

Without doubt the greatest that I played with was Bill Dean. He was an inspirational leader who didn't need to have the club's name tattooed on his arm - it was etched on his heart. Every team was intimidated by the mere mention of his name. Bill was so much better than his opponents that they would leave a unique aroma in their penalty area - the smell of fear. Tales of his behaviour on and off the pitch are legendary. Although I have always been a teetotaller, I know from first-hand experience that Bill could down a hat-trick of pints in the Winslow Hotel before kick-off and net a hat-trick of goals before half-time. He was an awesome gentleman as well as an awesome footballer and would go out of his way to help football fans of all persuasions. But you crossed him at your peril. I remember Bill was giving an interview on the edge of the pitch after training when an old groundsman demanded that the Everton star and his journalist friend get off his precious turf. He pointed to his battered sign which declared: *'Grass grows by the inch and dies by the foot!'* Of course, Bill co-operated but returned a little later to seek revenge. He marched to the centre-spot, dropped his trousers and left a steaming souvenir for the groundsman!

Without question, the most skilful player that I ever coached was Colin Harvey. He was pure class and deserved to be eulogised as 'The White Pelé'. Given his immaculate ball skills, I'm proud to think that I helped him improve his passing technique. But there again, I feel compelled to acknowledge some other great talents who I had under my wing at Bellefield like wee Bobby Collins, Brian Labone, Alex Parker, Alex Young and Roy Vernon. Of course, I could also reel off the names of other tremendously gifted footballers who wore the famous blue and white with pride but they are all profiled in this book. Instead, I would prefer to pay tribute to a few unsung heroes behind the scenes.

During my playing days the club was professionally run by dedicated Evertonians such as club chairman Will Cuff, whose iron grip also controlled the Football League, directors Jack Sharp, Ernest Green and Cecil Baxter, whose family's generosity effectively built Goodison Park, club secretaries Tom McIntosh and Theo Kelly, who made it their business to know every gate-man and every programme seller by name, and chief coach Harry Cooke, whose ice-cold sponge had magical as well as therapeutic properties. They were all true Blues and tremendous characters. Harry Cooke was aided by a blind masseur also named Harry Cook who developed the knack for recognising players by touch. He had no difficulty in identifying Bill Dean by his strong neck muscles, Tommy Lawton by his extra-long shins, Joe Mercer by his famous bandy gait and Albert Geldard by his very hairy torso. But 'Blind Harry' claimed that I had the ugliest back-side at Goodison!

Being employed by Everton Football Club was a very special honour. My last job was as a stadium tour-guide and it was like showing friends around my home. It wasn't a job - it was a real labour of love. Not surprisingly, having dedicated the best years of my life to the club, I detest the way in which we've been marginalised in recent years. In all honesty, I don't think that we've recovered from the death of Mr Moores. He brought more than a healthy bank balance to Goodison Park - he brought high standards and sound judgement. As a result, he raised everyone's ambitions. Of course, we can't live in the past but it seems to me that lots of loyal employees who shared his pride and expectations have been cast aside in recent years.

Messrs Moores and Cuff as well as the other Goodison gods must have been watching over me because I was discarded yet managed to land on my feet. For a start, I was privileged to be inducted into Gwladys Street's Hall of Fame in March 2000.

It is a genuine thrill for me to be included with such distinguished footballers. The Hall of Fame Gala was a truly magical evening. The atmosphere at the Adelphi Hotel made the hairs on the back of my neck stand up and the opportunity to meet royal blue stars from different generations, such as TG Jones, Wally Fielding, Dave Hickson, Alex Young, Howard Kendall, Paul Bracewell, Dave Watson as well as 600 other bluebloods, both young and old, has galvanised my pride in being an Evertonian. In fact, that wonderful evening gave me the desire to live for ever.

Nowadays, many people beyond the boundaries of Merseyside don't know about our history and crudely associate our name with bank overdrafts and relegation dog-fights. Let me advise the cynics among them that there is something very special about being an Evertonian. We've never been the flavour of the month or the band-wagon to be jumped on - but we are the first club of Merseyside and our traditions are second to none. Everton gets into your blood and never leaves. One huge banner at the Hall of Fame said it all: *'Once an Evertonian, Always an Evertonian.'*

Being an Evertonian equates to being a member of a very special family - brothers and sisters who are devoted to looking after their own. No other football club has established a registered charity to assist its old players overcome medical and other hardships. I speak from first-hand experience. I never asked for help, rather the Everton Former-Players' Foundation came to me because they genuinely cared about my welfare. I attended my first Hall of Fame event in a wheel-chair and shortly afterwards underwent surgery to replace my arthritic hip. It appears that my hip joint had disintegrated and, as a consequence, my left leg was some two inches shorter than my right. My operation was arranged by the Foundation and the Professional Footballers Association - and I'm indebted to the kindness of my fellow Evertonians for giving me a new lease on life. Twelve months later, I attended my second Hall of Fame Gala and the thrill of walking into the Adelphi's Banqueting Hall alongside some of the greatest names in the history of English football made this old blue-boy very happy.

From my experience in the game and the business of football, I strongly believe that Everton fans are different from others. Possibly it's our pride in our long history which makes us so special. More probably it's our inherent strength of character. In the late-Thirties, I remember an injured Bill Dean hobbling around the dressing room before my first derby game at Anfield. He put his arm around me and pointed to the shirts hanging from the hooks: *"Wear your jersey with pride. We don't need fancy badges to advertise who we are. Everyone knows that the team in blue and white playing entertaining football must be Everton. Every man, woman and child out there knows that Everton are special!"* And from his corner of the dressing room, Joe Mercer responded: *"Amen brother."*

Like Joe Mercer, I'm proud to share Bill Dean's love for Everton Football Club. But I worry about the future. When did Walter Smith's side last play in the Everton way? Everton football - has it become an oxymoron? No wonder Bill's statue has his back turned to the action at Goodison.

In sickness and in health, we are special - we always have been and always will be.

Gordon Watson

March 2001

Pedigree

Blyth Spartans
Everton

Born: 1914
Seghill

Blue Stats

	apps	goals
League	61	1
FA Cup	5	0
Other	193	1
Total	259	2
1936/37-48/49		

Anyone who had the privilege of being escorted around Goodison by him could not fail to be impressed by Gordon Watson's love for Everton. The club was the air that he had breathed for nearly 70 years. Gordon died in April 2001, one month after fulfiling his final ambition. Pushed into the Hall of Fame Gala Dinner in a wheelchair, he vowed to march into the following year's celebrations unaided after hip replacement surgery. Gordon did so to the sounds of 'Z Cars' with the FA Cup held high. There wasn't a dry eye among the 600 former-players and fans present. He was a gentleman - a champion - an Evertonian.

David France

Gordon Watson 5

Yes, yes, we'll deal with your lost Lowry in a moment ... but where on earth did you come by this picture of Danny Williamson with dirty knees?

It's Enough To Make Your Heart Go
... Wooo ooo oooh

Everton have woven a golden thread through the evolution of the English game and, as a result, the air around Goodison Park has always been thick with the fragrance of a rich and textured history. The first football club of Merseyside has enjoyed an unrivalled tenure of 100 seasons at the top and throughout this period Evertonians have sung the praises of many of football's favourite sons. Indeed, the story of Everton Football Club is the story of the men who shaped it. This book illuminates the exceptional contributions made by them.

Fans are often accused of living in the past but we believe that there is an acceptable face of nostalgia. The establishment of Gwladys Street's Hall of Fame in 1998 succeeded in honouring the club's icons as well as recognising the need to salute other influential characters of yesteryear before memories of their prowess fade forever. Because most history books have concentrated on the accomplishments of 'Dixie' Dean and the men who followed him, modern fans have developed a blind spot which appears to occlude the pioneers who bathed the club in success before the arrival of the greatest goal-scorer of all time. For example, many of the players from the nineteenth century seem to have been overlooked. John Douglas, Jack McGill, Tom Marriott, Mike Higgins, Dan Doyle and Nick Ross - all of them at one time or another were the toast of Merseyside and their names were embroidered into the early tapestry of the club. This book is designed to acknowledge the deeds of these unsung heroes as well as those of the superstars.

Everton's early quest for honours was commemorated in the book compiled by Thomas Keates in 1929 for the golden jubilee. However, an even older publication was recently discovered which chronicles the pioneering days in greater detail. Attributed to the quill of Floreat Evertonia, this eye-witness recollection of Everton's formative years was written only 15 years after the club's first recorded fixture in Stanley Park. In order to document the endeavours of the forgotten heroes, the original text is reproduced verbatim in the chapter called *Birth Of The Blues*. Our research failed to uncover other comprehensive sources of information detailing the embryonic years and, as a consequence, we tapped into the encyclopaedic knowledge of that great old man of Everton - Gordon Watson.

Given his unique qualification of a lifetime at Everton, his one and only League club, Gordon recounted individuals from the club's proud history. We weren't surprised by his intimate knowledge of all things blue. He had been perfectly placed to size up the men who had passed through the doors of Goodison and Bellefield and reassured us that he had kept his eyes and ears open for more than six decades. Indeed, if he had not known the men personally then he had known someone who had, even back to the very first days of St Domingo in Stanley Park. His appraisals were drawn from his word-of-mouth reminiscences with other dedicated club servants as well as his first-hand observations from his day-to-day life playing and training at Everton. Gordon had turned out alongside icons such as TG Jones and Joe Mercer for whom he could not find enough superlatives and had worked alongside venerable trainer Harry Cooke in coaching the likes of Bobby Collins and Alex Young. Equally as invaluable, he had earned the respect of long-term club officials such as Will Cuff, Jack Sharp and Theo Kelly.

There have been so many great players that we understood at the outset that even the compilation of a short-list of 201 individuals would be an arduous task and the subsequent profiles would be a formidable undertaking for anyone, let alone a senior citizen aged 87. Gordon's assessments are provided in the chapter headed *Gwladys Street's Family*. He also developed a 5-star rating system for comparing players from different eras.

Like most Blues, we had been weaned on tales of the School of Science as well as a few myths of the School of Science Fiction and thought that we were acquainted with the club's past - that is until we heard Gordon's vivid tales of the comings and goings at Goodison. It was an education in family genealogy. We listened to him for hours while he was convalescing from surgery and were captivated by his candour - often witty, sometimes scathing, occasionally cliched but always refreshingly eloquent. Gordon never lived in a sentimental time-warp believing that the game was always better in his day and, most important, strove to offer honest assessments while not wanting to betray or offend anyone.

Inducted into Gwladys Street's Hall of Fame in March 2000, Gordon agreed with the vast majority of the selections. However, he believed that there had been some oversights and thought that the doors of the Hall of Fame should be flung open to welcome Jack McGill, Harry Cooke, Jackie Coulter and Torry Gillick. He would often ask: "*How could the most knowledgeable football fans in the country forget about Coulter and Gillick? Don't they know their history? Any other club would have erected bronze statues to honour them.*"

Since its formation, Gwladys Street's Hall of Fame has grown from strength-to-strength into an enthusiastic celebration of royal blue pride. To qualify for membership, players and club officials must have made significant contributions to the welfare of Everton. Back in 1998, a panel of former-players, journalists, shareholders and season-ticket holders appraised the merits of the 750 or so players who had represented the club since the pioneering days of St Domingo's. No formal guidelines were provided in order that the appraisals embraced extraordinary feats. In keeping with the club's motto - Nil Satis Nisi Optimum - the likelihood of selection was low. At that time, 75 players and five club officials were selected for membership, each and every one of them sharing an unwavering commitment to Everton.

Possibly the standards of the Hall of Fame are best reflected in the qualifications of the well-known stars who have yet to be inducted. The merits of a few candidates are considered annually to correct any glaring omissions and reflect recent achievements and subsequent polls have elected 12 additional members. Others may be added through future ballots but, in the post-Bosman era, it is likely that few modern-day players will be elected to join the Goodison elite.

Ballot Year	Total Votes	Hall of Fame Inductees and % Total Votes					
1999	465	Paul Bracewell	22.2 %	Andy King	20.3 %	Gordon Watson	20.0 %
2000	1864	Derek Mountfield	25.9 %	Philip Carter	22.8 %	Duncan McKenzie	20.0 %
2001	2010	Barry Horne	27.1 %	Alex Scott	23.6 %	Jimmy Husband	22.8 %
2002	2236	Fred Pickering	21.1 %	Alan Whittle	20.2 %	Kevin Richardson	20.1 %

The real challenge in writing another book about Everton Football Club is to find language free from sentimental nostalgia and assertive paradox. Frankly, there can be no middle ground when it comes to loving Everton. It is much more than a football club - it is a state of mind. And like us, most Blues are guilty of wallowing in the exploits of our forefathers because, to put it bluntly, that is all that we've had for some time.

GWLADYS STREET'S ™
HALL of FAME

ESTABLISHED 1998

Walter Abbott	Alan Ball	Billy Balmer	Dr James Baxter
John Bell	Billy Bingham	Richard Boyle	Paul Bracewell
Cliff Britton	Sir Philip Carter	Mr Harry Catterick	Edgar Chadwick
Sam Chedgzoy	Bobby Collins	Billy Cook	Warney Cresswell
Mr Will Cuff	Dixie Dean	Jimmy Dunn	Tommy Eglington
Peter Farrell	Wally Fielding	Tom Fleetwood	Bertie Freeman
Jimmy Gabriel	Fred Geary	Charlie Gee	Albert Geldard
Andy Gray	Harold Hardman	Brian Harris	Hunter Hart
Colin Harvey	Adrian Heath	Dave Hickson	Johnny Holt
Barry Horne	John Hurst	Jimmy Husband	Tommy Jones
TG Jones	Howard Kendall	Roger Kenyon	Andy King
Brian Labone	Bob Latchford	Alex Latta	Tommy Lawton
Mike Lyons	Mr George Mahon	Harry Makepeace	Duncan McKenzie
Joe Mercer	Alf Milward	Sir John Moores	Johnny Morrissey
Derek Mountfield	Alex Parker	Bobby Parker	John Willie Parker
Fred Pickering	Kevin Ratcliffe	Peter Reid	Joe Royle
Kevin Richardson	Ted Sagar	Alex Scott	Billy Scott
Jimmy Settle	Graeme Sharp	Jack Sharp	Kevin Sheedy
Neville Southall	Jack Southworth	Jimmy Stein	Trevor Steven
Gary Stevens	Alex Stevenson	Jack Taylor	Derek Temple
Jock Thomson	Alec Troup	Roy Vernon	Dave Watson
Gordon Watson	Gordon West	Tommy White	Alan Whittle
Ray Wilson	Tommy Wright	Alex Young	Sandy Young

★ 2002

By his own admission, Gordon was a die-hard who, during the writing of this book, would often pause to vent his frustrations regarding the misery that has clouded recent seasons. At our first meeting back in 2000, he expressed his fear that Goodison was no longer alive with ambition and thought that it had been amusingly re-branded 'The Home of the Blues'. Another time, after recounting the exploits of Alex Young, he asked: *"What ever happened to our School of Science values? Don't today's players understand that our Latin motto is an oath?"* Ostensibly, Gordon tried to laugh through his pain of despair. After a particularly ugly performance, he mused: *"It's not just Walter Smith's fault. We're all in this together - but Everton are to football what Tinky Winky, Dipsy, Laa-Laa and Po are to drama."* He had become pessimistic - worrying that some fans maintained delusions of grandeur, believing that the club is a sleeping giant. He cautioned that while we did go to sleep as a giant in the wake of Heysel - we will be fortunate to wake up as one. He also believed that in the interim, while consoling ourselves that we will be lucky to see men of the calibre of 'The Golden Vision' any time soon, we must not settle for second best.

Blues should appreciate that Gordon relayed his feelings in the period immediately prior to the breath of fresh air that was David Moyes' arrival. But it is clear that in order to compete with the nouveau riche of the Premiership, we must maintain our strategic approach, or at least our disciplined 12-step programme, and not get too carried away with the buzz which has accompanied the precocious talents and broad shoulders of a certain young boy from De La Salle High School. It should go without saying that Gordon was not enamoured by many of those on the club's books in 2001. He claimed that as a child his mother had scolded him that if he couldn't say anything nice about someone then he should keep his mouth shut. Therefore, to avoid any unnecessary embarrassment, several well-respected old boys were invited to offer their objective assessments of Walter Smith's flock and David Moyes' subsequent additions in the chapter titled *Home Of The Blues*.

Gordon was aware that his views were jaundiced blue by obsession and considered others better qualified to tackle the darker side of the Hall of Fame - that is the shadowlands that shelter the poor souls who have worn royal blue without distinction. We concurred that it would be hurtful to label something a 'Hall of Shame', which sounded too much like a register of post-war reprobates who have committed some terrible crime against humanity, instead of being soccer misfits. Len Capeling of the *Daily Post* proposed the slightly critical ring of *Gone But Not Forgiven* for the heading of the final chapter.

Gordon had seen it all, having lived through two World Wars, dissolution of the British Empire, closure of the mines and the docks and, of course, several white-knuckle rides in Everton's fortunes, and it was an immense privilege for us to produce this book with him. We all wanted to create something really special - a bequest o the future generations of our royal blue family - and trust that our efforts have succeeded in keeping the flame alive.

'The People's Club' has enjoyed an unparalleled history. As Gwladys Street loves to sing: *"It's enough to make your heart go ... Wooo ooo oooh"*.

October 2002

*It was at the Park End ... Alec Troup's corner seemed to hang in the air
as the great man soared majestically above the Arsenal defence. It was sixty for Dixie!*

Birth Of The Blues

In presenting the public with anything approaching a detailed history of the Everton Football Club, the earlier chronicles of the organisation must naturally resolve themselves into a vague and shadowy form, as until the club began to make a prominent name for itself, its record and story were perhaps little worth recording. However, as far as authentic records carry us back, the year 1878 seems to be the first definite date where its chronicles commence. In that year the St Domingo Cricket Club, playing upon a plot of ground opposite the old Anfield cricket ground in Oakfield Road (and whose members chiefly consisted of the younger portion of the worshippers at the Congregational Chapel in St Domingo Vale) in order to keep themselves in training during the winter months, inaugurated a football team for Saturday afternoons' practice. No matches were arranged but those so disposed journeyed to Stanley Park and indulged in a little football exercise. Their play, of course, was of a most elementary character.

In the following year, 1879, the club was properly organised under the name of St Domingo Football Club. Matches were played against St Mary's, St Peter's, Everton United Church and Bootle St John's, which latter club became, and has existed until recently as, the Bootle Football Club. About November the members appeared dissatisfied with their club's name and, being ambitious of a more imposing one, at a meeting held at their then headquarters, Clarke's Queen's Head Hotel in Village Street, resolved unanimously to call their club 'The Everton Football Club', and Mr J Clarke was elected their first secretary.

The following month, December 23rd, the new club played its first match under its new name against St Peter's and scored their first success. In February 1880, Everton first met Bootle St John's at Stanley Park and even at that early date the match attracted a lot of local interest. During the summer months football was practiced quite as frequently as cricket and in the evening practices, preparing for the coming season, such famed players as M'Gill, Richards and Provan first had their talents discovered and appreciated, eventually joining the club.

Prior to the season 1880-81, the club's committee, aspiring to meeting more formidable opponents, obtained permission to enter the Lancashire Association, and in the cup contest following were drawn against the powerful Great Lever Football Club. In September they first met the newly-formed Liverpool Football Club and, as an omen for future years, Everton were victorious by three goals. The club's first serious travelling journey was to encounter the Great Lever Football Club above mentioned and, although anticipating a heavy defeat, were lucky enough to escape with a draw. On the occasion of the re-playing, however, Great Lever threw no chance away and won easily by 8 goals to 1. The club was not disheartened and as a result of their pluck and enterprise, won match after match until the Lancashire Association, noticing their ability, invited them to nominate M'Gill, and he was then selected to play for Lancashire against North Wales on January 31st 1881. His success in this match was so decided as to bring him prominently before the notice of his native county, Ayrshire, who elected him to represent them in February 1881. The annual meeting was held at the Queen's Head in June 1881 and among the officials elected, M'Gill became captain and Evans sub-captain.

At the commencement of the following season the club's costume was changed, having been blue and white stripes; but the number of players joining from other clubs, and each having colours of their own, they decided to dye them all black, and were worn with a scarlet sash across their shoulders, procuring for them, about that time, the name of 'Black Watch'.

This season opened disastrously, Bolton Wanderers defeating them by 13 to 1. They amply atoned for this, however, the week after when they defeated the then powerful Northwich Victoria by 2 to 0. This was their best achievement up to that date and brought the young Everton club into great prominence in the little football world. On December 11th Everton journeyed into another football stronghold to play Turton, the oldest and strongest club in the Association, and were only defeated 3 to 1. Even at this early date the officials recognised the coming prominence of the game and were anxious to secure a private ground, but local landlords were decidedly antagonistic to allowing their fields to be used for such a 'mad game'. Continual efforts at last met with a reward and, in March 1882, a general meeting of the members and friends was held at the Sandon Hotel (just opened) for the purpose of securing a suitable field and a sub-committee was formed with that object. The closing match of this season was between a selected team of Everton and a team of the Bootle club and resulted in one of the most enthusiastic matches of those days, Everton eventually winning by 7 to 4. Their record for this season was played 22, won 15, lost 3, drawn 4; scoring 70 goals against 16.

During the summer season the club was invited by the officials of the Stanley Hospital Gala to contribute some players to form a team representing Liverpool against Darwen, the match being played in Stanley Park during Whit-week. At the annual meeting on May 10th, the present director Mr R Wilson was then first elected as Vice-President of the club. The first match of importance in the following season, 1882-83, was with Blackburn Rovers, against whom Everton were drawn in the Lancashire Cup tie on October 2nd. The Rovers who were then the most powerful football club in existence, being easy winners by 8 to love. This match is perhaps unique in its way as affording the first local instance of 'poaching'. Mr S Ormrod, the present veteran referee and at that time a member of the Accrington club, was present and admiring M'Gill's play. He waylaid him after the match and convinced him that as a centre-forward for Accrington he would improve his position, and succeeded so well in his persuasion that for the following three months Everton knew the famous 'Jack' no more. It was at this date that the formation of a Liverpool Association was suggested, Mr Robert Lythgoe being one of the promoters, and the present organisation was then evolved.

On November 27th Everton again met Bootle and the latter club having many good players, won a hard game by 2 to 0. In January 1883, M'Gill returned from Accrington and assisted Everton to overcome the Liverpool Football Club in the local cup tie on January 8th by 8 to 0. Another most exciting match then took place between Everton and Bootle, and Bootle being again strongly supported by neighbouring clubs, the match resolved itself after a very hard game into a fiasco, Bootle maintaining they won and Everton claiming a draw, the match being unfinished. It is perhaps worth recording that at this date occurs the name of one of the more finished players of recent years, Brodie, the Wolverhampton and international player assisting Bootle. In the summer of 1883, the committee secured their first ground, Mr Cruitt of Coney Green, Anfield, lending his field in Priory Road, and the club's records show that their first gate income amounted to 14/-. It may interest the public to know that in those early days the team consisted of goal-keeper, two backs, two half-backs and six forwards. It is curious to note that in November 1883, a Mr J Trainer was elected a member of the club and was chosen to play in the second team, this player being none other than the famous North End goal-keeper of today and Welsh international. After his election he only remained some short time and then went to Bolton.

The end of this season, 1883-84, saw Everton defeat Earlestown in the final of the Liverpool Cup amidst tremendous excitement and enthusiasm, and the scene in the headquarters that evening will long be remembered, the club eventually receiving the Challenge Cup from the Association. The ensuing season raised the old difficulty about a ground, the landlord requiring his field, and it was not until August that, as a result of a deputation to Mr Orrell, they obtained their first ground in Anfield Road.

In those days members were enthusiastic enough to spend their spare time in filling up holes and levelling the ground, in order to prepare for the coming season, and on September 29th, being then entirely closed, it was opened with a match against Earlestown, who were defeated by five goals. Meeting Bootle in the Liverpool Cup tie, they drew a very big gate for those days, and after playing full time without scoring, amidst great excitement, the referee ordered extra time to be played, and after ten minutes play, Bootle scored the first goal. The enthusiasm was now intense and when, upon starting the last quarter's play, Whittle equalised, the cheering was tremendous, and upon Parry scoring the winning goal on the call of time, the wildest football scene of those days took place, and Parry was carried shoulder high from the field to the head-quarters. In the Final tie against Earlestown, however, an unpleasant dispute arose over a doubtful goal scored by Everton, and Earlestown were awarded the cup. We learn from the records that the club's income for the season then ended amounted to about £200, as compared with £45 the previous year.

At the general meeting in 1885, George Dobson was elected captain, and we notice amongst the players at this date George Farmer's name also, these being the first two professionals employed by the club. The Blackburn Rovers, the Blackburn Olympic, Accrington, Bolton Wanderers, &c. now began to find Everton as worthy of a visit in every sense, and in the season following, matches were arranged with them. This season was also very successful, the gates consistently increasing, and as a result of this, during the following season 1886-87, Smalley, Dick and Weir joined the club. At this date Scottish football was first introduced into Liverpool, the famous Glasgow Rangers of the present day paying their first visit in one of the National Cup ties, and only defeating Everton by one goal, after playing one of the finest games ever seen upon the ground. In December 1887, Everton were suspended by the English Association for two months, as a result of irregularities with Scotch players, Goudie, Murray and Cassady, who returned home in January 1888. This season saw the inauguration of the Football League and out of twelve clubs Everton obtained the eighth place, with 20 points.

The achievements of the team in the League up to the present time is:

Season	Clubs	Position	Points
1888-89	12	8	20
1889-90	12	2	31
1890-91	12	1	29
1891-92	14	5	28
1892-93	16	3	36
1893-94	16	6	33

At the Annual Meeting, we find the names of Ross, Holt and Chadwick first occurring as players of the club. For the season ending the record was played 70, won 40, lost 22, drew 8; goals for 149 against 105. In the following season, Mr R Molyneux, the present Secretary, first assumed his office, and the Reserve team being strengthened became known as 'Everton', the first team assuming the higher title of 'Everton League', and this season saw the advent to the club of Geary, Hannah, Doyle, Latta and Brady, and as a result of the high standard of play shown by the players the end of the season saw Everton taking second place with 31 points, Preston North End being champions with 33 points. The team at this date consisted of Smalley, Hannah, Doyle, Kirkwood, Holt, Parry, Latta, Brady, Geary, Chadwick and Milward.

The records of the following season are no doubt well known to all. We may mention that the team began by playing 13 matches without a loss, winning the League championship with a total of 29 points, and their total record for this season was played 46, won 38, lost 6, drew 2, scoring 148 to 35, which may be considered as a performance rarely eclipsed by any premier club before or since. The team that achieved these results consisted of Angus, Doyle, Hannah,

Kirkwood, Holt, Campbell, Latta, Brady, Geary, Chadwick and Milward. Of their latter history we may content ourselves with saying that the season 1891-92 saw them conclude with a record of played 62, won 31, lost 19, drew 12; goals for 137 against 100, the team consisting of Jardine, Collins, McLean, Kirkwood, Holt, Kelso, Latta, Gordon, Geary, Chadwick and Milward, and towards the close of the season, Williams, Earp, Howarth, Hope-Robertson and Wylie were included. It is not desirable to revert at this date to old and controversial matters so we may content ourselves with stating that the committee of the club found it desirable to enlarge their scope and accommodation for the increasing multitudes who now patronised the game, by removing to their present commodious ground at Goodison Park, and prior to the commencement of the season 1892-93, the members of the club who then numbered many hundreds formed themselves into a limited company under the chairmanship of Mr G Mahon, the first Directors being Messrs Clayton, Griffiths, Atkinson, Currier, Jackson, Coates, Davies, Leyland and Dr Baxter. Their subscribed capital was fixed at £2500 and the result of their financial operations since can be seen by a reference to the club's balance sheet.

The season ending 1893, under the management of the new company, resulted in the club reaching the Final tie for the English Cup, after defeating North End in the semi-final at the third attempt, only to be in turn vanquished by the Wolverhampton Wanderers at Fallowfield by one goal to nil, this match drawing an amount in gate money that has never been equalled by any cup tie record before or since. The record for this season was played 62, won 32, lost 18, drew 12: goals for 147 against 108, the team at the end of the season consisting of Williams, Kelso, Howarth, Boyle, Holt, A Stewart, Latta, Gordon, Geary, Chadwick and Milward, and one of the final matches of this year, played on Easter Monday, saw the inclusion of J Bell, the famous Dumbarton and international player.

Of their achievements in the season just ended, little remains to be said, the result being fresh in the minds of all readers. We may, however, close by saying that the record was played 59, won 35, lost 19, drew 5: goals for 173 against 93. The club is perhaps unique in the possession at the present time of 12 international players, viz, Adams, Arridge, Parry, Kelso, Boyle, Holt, Latta, Bell, Southworth, Geary, Chadwick and Milward, and with other players engaged such as R Williams, Cain, Walker, Storrier, Reay, Hartley, McInnes, Murray, W Williams, McMillan and Elliott, it is not too much to hope that the season now commencing will enhance the prominent position which the club has obtained in days gone by.

Income	£	s	d	Expenditure	£	s	d
Gate receipts	7769	0	7	Players' wages and bonuses	4213	2	0
Proceeds of matches played away	535	16	4	Amount paid visiting clubs	1233	10	9
Season tickets	560	10	6	Travelling expenses	538	2	9
Profit on special excursion tickets	15	15	3	Advertising, billposting, and stationery	402	18	10
Advertising contractor -				Gate expenses and checkers	245	19	0
for programmes and hoarding	160	0	0	Training expenses and trainer's wages	268	8	3
for refreshments	25	0	0	Ground expenses	366	19	0
Transfer fees	7	6	6	Twelve months' rent of ground	50	0	0
Player's insurance recovered for injuries	45	0	0	Rates, water, gas, telephone, &c.	132	1	7
	9118	9	2	Income tax	55	3	0
				Office expenses, postage, &c.	212	8	5
				Clothing, stores and stable expenses	233	9	2
				Medical fees and players' insurance	56	18	5
				League, &c. subscriptions and donations	39	17	0
				Entertaining visiting clubs	10	16	3
				Sundry expenses	40	11	9
				Law costs and auditors' fees	42	13	4
				Balance carried to profit and loss account	975	9	8
					9118	9	2

For year ending April 30th 1894

Prior to settling on royal blue in 1901, Everton wore shirts of many different colours and many different styles.

Alan Ball ... Alan Ball ... I distinctly said Alan Ball.

Gwladys Street's Family

International appearances
during Everton career

👑 England: 1 cap

Pedigree

Small Heath
Everton
Burnley
Birmingham

**Born: 1877
Birmingham**

Blue Stats

	apps	goals
League	257	32
FA Cup	34	5
Other	0	0
Total	291	37

1899/1900-07/08

Walter Abbott was 'The Beast of Walton-on-the-Hill'. Jack Sharp told me that Abbott was the most intimidating player in the great Everton sides which put the club's name on the map at the turn-of-the-century. He was the Tony Kay of his day - in that, no-one messed with him. The England half-back was a big lad with a kick like a mule and, from all accounts, didn't care too much about what or who he kicked. His reputation was cemented when he covered every blade of grass to ensure that we won the FA Cup for the first time in 1906. There was said to be a daunting Old Testament air about him that day at The Crystal Palace. ★★★★ **Gordon Watson**

Pedigree

Liverpool
Derby County (loan)
Hull City (loan)
Everton
Sheffield United (loan)
Birmingham City
Blackpool
Long Island Rough Riders

Born: 1965
Liverpool

Blue Stats

	apps	goals
League	128	5
FA Cup	12	1
Other	16	1
Total	156	7
1991/92-95/96		

Gary Ablett enjoys a unique place in Merseyside folklore - he is the only player to have gained FA Cup winners' medals with both Everton and Liverpool. Ablett was a no-frills, no-thrills defender who was never totally accepted by the Goodison fans. I thought that he sometimes laboured at full-back and was more influential in the middle of the back-four slotting smoothly alongside Dave Watson. With all due respect to Ablett, he isn't usually mentioned in the same breath as Watson. His finest hour was in the semi-final against Spurs when he clipped over an inch-perfect cross for Daniel Amokachi to net our third goal.

★ **Gordon Watson**

International appearances
during Everton career

♛ Nigeria: 12 caps

Pedigree

Ranchiers Bees
Club Brugge
Everton
Besiktas
Colorado Rapids
Emirates

Born: 1973
Groko, Nigeria

Blue Stats

	apps	goals
League	34/9	10
FA Cup	2/3	3
Other	6	1
Total	42/12	14
1994/95-95/96		

Daniel Amokachi was our first African Blue and expectations were sky-high when Mike Walker purchased the muscular striker for a colossal fee. It was a very ambitious signing by a very desperate manager. To be honest, I've always thought that there was something odd about the alleged 21 year-old - like the candles cost more than the cake at his birthday party. 'Amo' never adjusted to the Premiership climate - his first touch let him down. It was woeful and, as they say, his second touch was a tackle. His marksmanship was equally erratic but I'll never forget his unbridled glee after scoring two goals against Spurs at Elland Road.   ★ **Gordon Watson**

International appearances
during Everton career

👑 Wales: 3 caps

Pedigree

Bangor
Bootle
Everton
New Brighton Tower

Born: 1870
Sunderland

Blue Stats

	apps	goals
League	51	0
FA Cup	5	0
Other	0	0
Total	56	0
1893/94-96/97		

Smart Arridge - what a great first name! The left-back was more rugged than his contemporaries and added a bit of devil to the Everton rearguard. He was encouraged to soften up opposing wingers in the opening minutes with his fearsome shoulder charges and other biting challenges. Arridge was known to be a nasty little sod but is best remembered for his acrimonious exit. Like Ted Critchley and Fred Pickering many years later, he'd played a key role in the early rounds but was unfairly overlooked for the FA Cup final against Aston Villa in 1897. As a result, Arridge Dubbined his boots and crossed the water to New Brighton.   ★ Gordon Watson

Pedigree

Blackburn Rovers
Everton
Newcastle United
Bristol City

Born: 1957
Liverpool

Blue Stats

	apps	goals
League	171	3
FA Cup	22	0
Other	27/2	0
Total	220/2	3
1979/80-85/86		

John Bailey made me chuckle. The lovable jester was a marvellous addition to the Everton defence as well as the dressing room. 'Bails' always radiated a sunny disposition and his self-depreciating banter was capable of lifting spirits especially in times of dire adversity. And to be fair, he was given plenty of opportunities to do so during Gordon Lee's time at the helm. 'Bails' was also a very tidy left-back who was at ease on the ball. At his very best, he had a trace of Ray Wilson about him. I thought that he was desperately unlucky to be replaced by Pat van den Hauwe, a less cultured defender, at the dawn of the glory years. ★★ **Gordon Watson**

International appearances
during Everton career

England: 39 caps

Pedigree

Blackpool
Everton
Arsenal
Southampton
Philadelphia Fury
Vancouver Whitecaps
Blackpool
Southampton
Bristol Rovers
Bulova

Born: 1945
Farnworth

Blue Stats

	apps	goals
League	208	66
FA Cup	21	5
Other	21	7
Total	250	78
1966/67-71/72		

Alan Ball is one of the immortals of the beautiful game. He combined precocious skills, including an absolutely sublime first-touch, with unbelievable industry. 'Bally' refused to accept defeat and, not surprisingly, didn't make too many friends on the pitch. His tremendous desire to win often resulted in him telling his team-mates as well as referees how to do their jobs. Without question 'Bally' was the best midfielder of his era and, no matter what the reasons, his Hummel boots shouldn't have been allowed to leave. Years later I bumped into him in Majorca and he confided that he'd never wanted to go. 'Bally' was simply irreplaceable. ★★★★★ **Gordon Watson**

Pedigree

Everton

Born: 1882
Liverpool

Blue Stats

	apps	goals
League	165	0
FA Cup	23	0
Other	0	0
Total	188	0
1903/04-11/12		

After contesting the left-back berth with Jack Crelley, Robert Balmer finally forced his way into the first-team picture and formed a cohesive partnership with his brother. The Balmer siblings went on to feature in 60 or so games together including the 1907 FA Cup final defeat. Will Cuff questioned whether young Balmer had fully recovered from injury to play in that important game. Overshadowed by his brother, he was something of a feather-weight who constantly punched above his weight. Indeed, Balmer was infamous for his rudimentary approach which included lashing the ball up field with token regard for its final destination. ★ **Gordon Watson**

International appearances
during Everton career

England: 1 cap

Pedigree

Aintree Church
South Shore
Everton
Croydon Common

Born: 1877
Liverpool

Blue Stats

	apps	goals
League	293	1
FA Cup	38	0
Other	0	0
Total	331	1
1897/98-1907/08		

Billy Balmer was the older of 'The Original Blues Brothers' and was the one to gain England international honours. He was a solid full-back who was equally as happy on either flank. Jack Sharp told me that Balmer was far from the prettiest of footballers but could be relied upon to make rock-hard tackles and hefty clearances in the family tradition. He knew how to take care of business and would sharpen the nails protruding from his leather studs before every contest. Balmer, one of Sharp's team-mates in the 1906 FA Cup-winning side, was said to have been extremely disappointed not to have gained any additional silverware. ★★ **Gordon Watson**

Dr Baxter was a devoted Evertonian who served as a club official for almost 40 years. Unlike some modern-day directors, Dr Baxter never hesitated to put his money where his mouth was. His interest-free loan underwrote the moonlight flit from Anfield and enabled the club to relocate to Goodison Park. His continued generosity made it possible for Everton to attract better players and establish a world-wide reputation for cultured play. Dr Baxter was a devout Roman Catholic and his son Cecil, a director during my playing days, hinted that there were mumblings that the ground move had undertones of religion mixed with temperance. ★★★★ **Gordon Watson**

Dr James Baxter

Pedigree

Carlisle United
Vancouver Whitecaps
Manchester United
Newcastle United
Liverpool
Everton
Newcastle United
Bolton Wanderers
Manchester City
Fulham
Hartlepool United

Born: 1961
Newcastle upon Tyne

Blue Stats

	apps	goals
League	81	25
FA Cup	4	1
Other	10	6
Total	95	32
1991/92-92/93		

Evertonians are indebted to Graeme Souness. In the summer of 1991, the red ring-master signed Dean Saunders and we gratefully picked up the redundant Peter Beardsley. The latter had been one of the most talented footballers of his day and proved to be an inspired addition. Even at age 30, Beardsley quickly converted the Goodison sceptics with his spectacular dribbling and razor-sharp marksmanship. He revelled in the hole behind the main strikers to the point of being a little too clever for some of them. To my utter amazement, Beardsley was allowed to move on to St James's Park after only two seasons. ★★★ **Gordon Watson**

International appearances
during Everton career

 Scotland: 3 caps

Pedigree

Dumbarton
Everton
Celtic
New Brighton Tower
Everton
Preston North End

**Born: 1870
Dumbarton**

Blue Stats

	apps	goals
League	177	62
FA Cup	22	8
Other	0	0
Total	199	70

1892/93-97/98 & 1901/02-02/03

John Bell was the chairman of the first player's union. However, Will Cuff was mortified by Bell's inclination to speak his mind and branded him a militant trouble-maker during the first of his two terms at Everton. Apparently, Bell had voiced his moral objections to pro footballers being bought and sold like prized heffers. He became a thorn in the side of the powers-that-be but his outbursts were tolerated because Bell was, first and foremost, a master dribbler renowned for his flair for the unusual. The former wonder-boy of Scottish football also found the net regularly and was credited with the first-ever goal in a Merseyside derby. ★★★★ **Gordon Watson**

Pedigree

Lowton St Mary's
Wigan Athletic
Everton

Born: 1915
Leigh

Blue Stats

	apps	goals
League	110	17
FA Cup	15	0
Other	214	54
Total	339	71
1935/36-48/49		

Stan Bentham and TG Jones are the only other surviving champions from 1939. Stan was a foot-soldier who toiled diligently in the midfield trenches without fanfare. He was constructive when in possession of the ball and tigerish in trying to recover it. His playing career spanned World War II before he joined me behind the scenes for another dozen seasons. Stan was also an excellent coach who again never received the praise that his dedication warranted. In those days the backroom staff had to turn their hands to anything. For example if we found tatty socks in the skip, we were expected to take them home to be darned. ★★★ **Gordon Watson**

Pedigree

Stoke City
Everton
Oldham Athletic

Born: 1948
Shrewsbury

Blue Stats

	apps	goals
League	139/8	8
FA Cup	9/1	0
Other	12/1	0
Total	160/10	8
1972/73-76/77		

Mike Bernard was bought to replace Alan Ball but couldn't fit into the shirt never mind the white boots of the maestro. Harry Catterick gambled most of the mammoth fee received from Arsenal on the midfielder - and lost. To his credit, Bernard was a competent ball-winner and some even claimed that he was unlucky not to receive international honours. Whereas I echo the views of the majority who considered him far too chunky to enhance our style of play. To be brutally frank, I thought he was something of a toffee pudding. Bernard took the path of other big buys such as Henry Newton and Ian Snodin and was reincarnated as a full-back.

★ **Gordon Watson**

International appearances
during Everton career

 Northern Ireland: 12 caps

Pedigree

Glentoran
Sunderland
Luton Town
Everton
Port Vale

Born: 1931
Belfast

Blue Stats

	apps	goals
League	86	23
FA Cup	7	2
Other	5	1
Total	98	26
1960/61-62/63		

Billy Bingham was a class-act who helped us carry off the championship in 1963. I reckoned that the veteran flankman reserved his most inspirational performances for his country. In fact, the distinguished Ulsterman advised me that I'd never heard the British national anthem until I'd experienced it resonating around Windsor Park. And he was right. Billy was also blessed with the gift of the gab and was keen to impart his wealth of experiences to his younger team-mates. Many years later he was charged with rebuilding the club after Harry Catterick's illness. Billy was given plenty of money but not enough time to find the right blend.　★★★　**Gordon Watson**

International appearances
during Everton career

England: 1 cap

Pedigree

Ashton North End
Blackburn Rovers
Everton
Preston North End
Carlisle United

Born: 1874
Manchester

Blue Stats

	apps	goals
League	175	9
FA Cup	10	2
Other	0	0
Total	185	11
1900/01-07/08		

Tom Booth plied his trade with quiet efficiency and rarely had an off-day. By all accounts, he was one of the most consistent pivots of his generation and represented both England and the Football League. I gather that Booth was similar in style to Brian Labone - that is, an elegant defender who relied on the timing of his tackles to dispossess opponents instead of brute force. He preferred to leave the rough stuff to Walter Abbott. Booth was also well-respected as an enthusiastic club captain who came tantalisingly close to collecting the game's top honours. Unfortunately, injuries forced him to miss back-to-back FA Cup finals. ★★ **Gordon Watson**

International appearances
during Everton career

England: 2 caps

Pedigree

Woodhouse Mills United
West Bromwich Albion
Everton
Notts County
Scunthorpe United
Retford Town

**Born: 1913
Sheffield**

Blue Stats

	apps	goals
League	66	11
FA Cup	7	4
Other	0	0
Total	73	15
1937/38-48/49		

Wally Boyes was a dirminutive winger but few full-backs could live with his quick feet. At 5 ft 3 in on his tip-toes, 'Curly' was the same height as Alex Stevenson and the two canny fellows ran defenders ragged with their intricate play. They were peas from the same pod. I was particularly impressed by 'Curly's' exquisite control because he was handicapped by having one peg much shorter than the other. He also netted a few goals during our championship triumph but I must admit that I grew tired of hearing about his 17 goals in one game as a schoolboy. Surely, there must be room in the Hall of Fame for another little one. ★★★ **Gordon Watson**

Pedigree

Dumbarton Episcopalians
Dumbarton Union
Dumbarton
Everton
Dundee

Born: 1870
Dumbarton

Blue Stats

	apps	goals
League	222	7
FA Cup	21	1
Other	0	0
Total	243	8
1892/93-1900/01		

Richard Boyle was one of the most influential captains in the early days. Will Cuff often boasted that Boyle had been the club's tuning fork: *"When wee Dickie was on song - the Toffees sang from the same hymn-sheet."* Everton plundered him from Dumbarton along with the pick of their Scottish championship-winning team. The right-half found Goodison to be the ideal stage for his creative passes and matured into the architect behind our teams in the late-nineteenth century. Inexplicably, the major honours of the English game eluded him. He skippered Everton in two FA Cup finals but was on the losing side on both occasions.   ★★★★ **Gordon Watson**

International appearances during Everton career

👑 England: 3 caps

Pedigree

Stoke City
Sunderland
Everton
Sunderland
Newcastle United
Fulham

Born: 1962
Heswall

Blue Stats

	apps	goals
League	95	7
FA Cup	19/2	0
Other	28/1	3
Total	142/3	10
1984/85-88/89		

Paul Bracewell had the type of talent that belonged at Goodison Park and was a magnificent midfield complement to Peter Reid. They were the ideal amalgam of skills and their ball-winning tackles, slick passes and inexhaustible stamina were the catalyst for our success in the 1980s. Sadly, 'Brace' never fully recovered from an ankle injury received in an appalling tackle by Billy Whitehurst at Newcastle and, as a consequence, was side-lined for two seasons. He was a great loss to his club and his country but remained a gentleman throughout his ordeal. 'Brace' is one of the most charming young men I've ever met.   ★★★★ **Gordon Watson**

International appearances
during Everton career

 England: 9 caps

Blue Stats

	apps	goals
League	221	2
FA Cup	19	1
Other	9	1
Total	249	4
1930/31-43/44		

Cliff Britton was a world-class half-back with a passing technique second to none. His creative game was made up of a short pass here, a longer calibrated pass there, a nifty flick of inspiration here, a rapier-thrust there. However, I don't think that Cliff ever forgave me for squeezing him out of the championship run-in. There again, I've never forgiven him for condemning our great club to three seasons in Division 2. Certainly, the hype that had preceded his appointment as general manager in 1948 went unfulfilled. His job was compounded by his own snooty desire to be revered in a god-like manner by all and sundry. ★★★★★ **Gordon Watson**

Pedigree

Partick Thistle
Everton
Shrewsbury Town
Southport
Fleetwood

**Born: 1939
Grangemouth**

Blue Stats

	apps	goals
League	176/35	9
FA Cup	16/8	0
Other	16/2	2
Total	208/45	11
1962/63-70/71		

'Sandy' Brown was a fine athlete who would play anywhere for the club that he loved. I had a lot of time for this proud club-man because he simply got on with his job and never complained. Primarily a full-back, he also played up-front and even between the sticks in times of crisis. While he always did his best, 'Sandy' will never be forgotten for his headed own-goal against the Reds. His howler confirmed that the gods of football may not be fair but do have a sense of humour. However, I prefer to recall the professional manner in which he poleaxed Johnny Giles during the infamously bad-tempered affair with Leeds in 1964.   ★★ **Gordon Watson**

Blue Stats

	apps	goals
League	128/7	10
FA Cup	7	1
Other	14	1
Total	149/7	12
1971/72-77/78		

Mick Buckley was cast from the same mould as Colin Harvey. And I can pay him no finer compliment. He'd been the glittering star of the England youth team which won the Little World Cup in 1972 and should have been groomed to take over from 'Bally'. I was an ardent fan of Buckley. He was an assertive competitor who could grab a game by the scruff of the neck. I still find it hard to accept that he was allowed to languish in the perennially under-performing outfits managed by Billy Bingham and Gordon Lee and was discarded to Roker Park when only 24. Perhaps he was pushed too far, too soon by Everton. ★★★ **Gordon Watson**

Pedigree

**Stockport County
Everton
Crewe Alexandra**

**Born: 1919
Darlington**

Blue Stats

	apps	goals
League	59	19
FA Cup	12	5
Other	73	56
Total	144	80
1939/40-51/52		

Harry Catterick would have walked over his own mother to have got what he wanted. I knew him as a team-mate and also worked for him as a coach. Although he made only a modest impact in the Number 9 shirt immediately after the war, Harry was a revelation as the club's manager in the Swinging Sixties. 'The Cat' was a hard task-master and was renowned for cloak and dagger deals as well as for grooming local lads. He wasn't trusted by everyone but enjoyed a decade of success - comparable to that of Bill Shankly. For some reason his accomplishments have not been recognised outside of the North West. ★★★★★ **Gordon Watson**

International appearances
during Everton career

 England: 7 caps

Pedigree

Little Dots
Blackburn Olympic
Blackburn Rovers
Everton
Burnley
Southampton
Liverpool
Blackpool
Glossop
Darwen

**Born: 1869
Blackburn**

Blue Stats

	apps	goals
League	270	97
FA Cup	30	13
Other	0	0
Total	300	110
1888/89-98/99		

Will Cuff claimed that Edgar Chadwick was his first hero which really isn't surprising since the inside-left was one of the household names of Victorian football. Recruited to strengthen our inaugural League crusade, he was famed for his blistering foot speed and his telepathic understanding with Alf Milward. The pair were considered the best in the business. Chadwick was a prominent member of our first team to win the title and also revered for his endeavours on the international stage. He grabbed a breathtaking goal shortly after the kick off of the Scotland-England game in 1892 - without a Scot touching the ball. ★★★★ **Gordon Watson**

International appearances
during Everton career

England: 8 caps

Pedigree

Burnell's Iron Works
Everton

**Born: 1890
Ellesmere Port**

Blue Stats

	apps	goals
League	279	33
FA Cup	21	3
Other	38	6
Total	338	42
1910/11-25/26		

Sam Chedgzoy was my boyhood idol and I was the proud owner of one of his cigarette cards. If my memory serves me well, he was photographed wearing an England cap embroidered with a Tudor rose. The outside-right initially hit the national headlines during the 1915 championship triumph, when he made the most of his pace and control to lay on a heap of goals for dazzling Bobby Parker, and was the most-feared winger in the game until his career was severely disrupted by World War I. Sam later emigrated to North America but never betrayed his love for the Toffees. He even came to cheer us during our 1948 tour. ★★★★★ **Gordon Watson**

Blue Stats

	apps	goals
League	46/11	18
FA Cup	2/8	0
Other	6/2	4
Total	54/21	22
1986/87-87/88		

I liked Wayne Clarke but as an instinctive marksman he wasn't a patch on Allan Clarke, his famous older brother. There again, very few were. Clarke was an honest player with a good eye for an opening and made a meaningful contribution to the 1986/87 championship campaign. In fact, he scored several vital goals for Everton - including one which drove a stake through the hearts of Kopites. After the Goodison bubble had burst, Clarke was somewhat rashly sacrificed in the part-exchange deal which gave us Mike Newell from Leicester. In retrospect, it definitely wasn't one of our best bits of wheeling and dealing.　　★　**Gordon Watson**

International appearances
during Everton career

 Northern Ireland: 12 caps

Pedigree

Portadown
Wolverhampton Wanderers
Coventry City
Sheffield Wednesday
Everton
New York Cosmos

Born: 1945
Larne

Blue Stats

	apps	goals
League	81/4	6
FA Cup	6	2
Other	8/1	1
Total	95/5	9

1973/74-75/76

Dave Clements enjoyed an illustrious career alongside some of the icons of world football such as Pelé with New York Cosmos and George Best with Northern Ireland. Obviously, he had to adjust his game at Everton where his team-mates included 'Dai the Drop' Davies and 'Tiger' McLaughlin. Clements was a strong midfielder capable of dictating the rhythm of proceedings. His approach was based on crisp tackling, accurate passing and astute reading of the game. Regrettably, Clements wasn't the most mobile of players. While he couldn't turn on a sixpence, it would be unfair to say that milk turned quicker than him.   ★★★   **Gordon Watson**

Blue Stats

	apps	goals
League	68	30
FA Cup	6	3
Other	114	104
Total	188	137
1913/14-21/22		

Joe Clennell was the artful dodger who gobbled up the knock-downs from Bobby Parker. Jack Sharp said that defenders found the Clennell-Parker strikeforce to be unstoppable and that Clennell was almost the equal of his famous partner. The inside-left was a potent predator and set out his stall by netting a hat-trick on the opening day of the 1914/15 championship season at Tottenham. Many fans thought that he'd stood on the threshold of greatness until his prospects were ruined by the outbreak of World War I. Clennell still retained his appetite for goals and scored over 100 times in war-time competitions for Everton. ★★ **Gordon Watson**

International appearances
during Everton career

Eire: 3 caps

Pedigree

Dundalk
Everton
Blackburn Rovers
Tranmere Rovers

Born: 1926
Dublin

Blue Stats

	apps	goals
League	73	4
FA Cup	7	1
Other	0	0
Total	80	5
1948/49-53/54		

Tommy Clinton was part of the Irish colony who had infiltrated Goodison by the early 1950s. Theo Kelly bragged that he'd signed the robust right-back through a train carriage window at Dundalk station. Tommy played most of his games in Division Two but is infamous for one game in the FA Cup - he missed a penalty in the 1953 semi-final. With keeper Stan Hanson frozen to the Maine Road turf, he calmly stroked the ball wide. It was a crucial miss because we fought back from 4-0 down to lose by the odd goal. The fans got over the set-back but his team-mates never did and we sank to an all-time low - sixteenth in Division Two. ★ **Gordon Watson**

Tommy Clinton

Pedigree

Brentford
Huddersfield Town
Chelsea
Everton
Plymouth Argyle
Millwall
Folkestone

Born: 1893
Hayle

Blue Stats

	apps	goals
League	69	29
FA Cup	3	2
Other	0	0
Total	72	31
1922/23-24/25		

Jack Cock was quite a controversial celebrity in the Roaring Twenties. After being reported missing-in-action during World War I, he eventually surfaced to be decorated with a bevy of military medals. As a centre-forward, the established England international was commended for his ball control and forged a productive alliance with Bobby Irvine at Everton. However, he had his critics. Club secretary Tom McIntosh wasn't overly-impressed by Cock's vanity and tagged him a flamboyant Southern dandy preoccupied with his appearance both on and off the pitch. Fittingly, Cock ventured into show business after leaving football. ★ **Gordon Watson**

International appearances
during Everton career

Scotland: 6 caps

Pedigree

Celtic
Everton
Leeds United
Bury
Morton
Hakoah
Oldham Athletic

**Born: 1931
Glasgow**

Blue Stats

	apps	goals
League	133	42
FA Cup	9	5
Other	5	1
Total	147	48
1958/59-61/62		

Wee Bobby Collins was one of the all-time greats. He was a crackerjack of a player who had great skills and the football brain to go with them. 'The Little General' was admired for his exquisite passing and tireless running and also feared for being a ravenous piranha in the tackle. Believe me, Bobby wasn't shy to put his foot in. He almost single-handedly saved us from the dreaded drop in 1959 and was the spring-board for our success in the Sixties. In my opinion, his twinkling size 4 boots were off-loaded in haste. To rub salt into Harry Catterick's wounds, Bobby was elected Footballer of the Year after his move to Leeds. ★★★★★ **Gordon Watson**

International appearances
during Everton career

Scotland: 6 caps

Pedigree

Celtic
Monaco
Everton
Fulham

Born: 1968
Galasheils

Blue Stats

	apps	goals
League	52/3	3
FA Cup	4	0
Other	3/2	1
Total	59/5	4
1998/99-1999/2000		

John Collins was a neat play-maker with a huge reputation - and an even bigger pay packet. He was signed as the European beacon of hope capable of putting the F back into EFC. After the early razzamataz had subsided, Collins struggled to adjust to the pace of the English game. In all honesty, I can't remember one game in which he imposed himself on those around him or for that matter got his kit dirty. Perhaps he arrived at the club at the wrong time because his passing skills appeared to be a luxury as we fought for Premiership survival. Whatever the excuse, he definitely wasn't a Bobby Collins - more a Joan Collins. ★ **Gordon Watson**

International appearances
during Everton career

Scotland: 1 cap

Pedigree

St Johnstone
Everton
Birmingham City
Newcastle United
Hibernian
Gateshead
Blyth Spartans
Gateshead

**Born: 1950
Barrhead**

Blue Stats

	apps	goals
League	105/3	15
FA Cup	3/1	0
Other	4	0
Total	112/4	15
1971/72-75/76		

I was a huge admirer of John Connolly. He was one of Harry Catterick's final acquisitions and I wasn't surprised to learn that the manager had left his sick-bed to sign the fabulously talented forward. Connolly possessed a repertoire of twists and turns akin to the great Jackie Coulter and would bring Goodison to its feet as he ran rings around bemused defenders. He could either ghost by or jink past or nutmeg them before arrowing crosses towards Bob Latchford. Cruelly, his bright future was devastated when he broke his leg during his Scotland debut. On a personal note, I'm impressed that he went on to play for Blyth Spartans. ★★★★ **Gordon Watson**

International appearances
during Everton career

Northern Ireland: 12 caps

Pedigree

Celtic
Everton
Wrexham

**Born: 1909
Coleraine**

Blue Stats

	apps	goals
League	225	5
FA Cup	24	1
Other	100	11
Total	349	17
1932/33-43/44		

Billy Cook was a very dangerous so-and-so with a very short fuse. Equally at home at right-back or left-back, he was one of the most formidable defenders of my generation. No battle was too small or too big for him. Nothing at all seemed to intimidate him. Billy possessed a callous streak and opponents would go weak at the knees when he simply winked at them. I knew him well because he was my room-mate for a time, not by choice, and I can report that he could've snored as well as drank ale for Northern Ireland. After the war he coached in Peru and Norway. I can't imagine what the Incas or the Vikings made of him! ★★★★ **Gordon Watson**

Pedigree

Everton

Born: 1882
Liverpool

Blue Stats

	apps	goals
League	7	3
FA Cup	2	0
Other	0	0
Total	9	3
1905/06		

Harry Cooke dedicated his life to Everton. He'd been twelfth man for the 1906 FA Cup final but shortly afterwards his playing days were cut down by injury. He latched on to the coaching staff and was eventually burdened with everything bar team selection. Harry was no nincompoop and let the old hands do their own thing on matchdays. It was a wise move because his training regime was bizarre - he'd only get the ball out on Tuesdays. He later concentrated on improving our fitness, relying on his magic sponge as well as his yarns about by-gone days to cure our ailments. 'Old Cookie' should be a corner-stone of the Hall of Fame.　★★★★　**Gordon Watson**

International appearances
during Everton career

 England: 4 caps

Pedigree

West Ham United
Everton
West Ham United
Manchester City
Selangor
Birmingham City
Leicester City
Norwich City
Barnet

Born: 1965
London

Blue Stats

	apps	goals
League	161/23	72
FA Cup	15/6	4
Other	19/4	11
Total	195/33	87
1988/89-94/95		

Tony Cottee was a big buy from West Ham and an even bigger disappointment. 'TC' had been acclaimed by the London press for his sharp-shooting and instinctive positioning but, in my opinion, suffered from chronic agoraphobia. I've always surmised that his arrival coincided with the end of our halcyon years. Cottee entered Goodison with all guns blazing and coolly blasted a hat-trick on his debut. It was an aberration because he failed to deliver consistent firepower before his return to Upton Park. By that time his value had plummeted so drastically that the deal involved a straight swop for ex-Red David Burrows.　　　★ **Gordon Watson**

International appearances
during Everton career

♛ Northern Ireland: 5 caps

Pedigree

Cliftonville
Belfast Celtic
Everton
Grimsby Town
Swansea Town
Chelmsford United

Born: 1912
Whiteabbey

Blue Stats

	apps	goals
League	50	16
FA Cup	8	8
Other	0	0
Total	58	24
1933/34-37/38		

Jackie Coulter was a wizard who illuminated every game in which he played. The unorthodox outside-left exhibited magical skills as well as electrifying pace. I'd go as far as to proclaim that he'd caress the ball with the tenderness of a mother's kiss before exploding into action moments later. Jackie did things with the ball that I hadn't believed a player could get away with in a competitive match. Gwladys Street adored him in a manner reserved for the chosen few. He continued to mesmerise defences until he fractured a leg when on international service. Those who saw Jackie Coulter play will never ever forget him. ★★★★★ **Gordon Watson**

Blue Stats

	apps	goals
League	116	0
FA Cup	11	0
Other	0	0
Total	127	0
1899/00-1907/08		

Jack Crelley was one of football's first nomads. The gritty defender drifted around the fledgling Southern League in search of employment before returning home to make a name for himself. Initially, he experienced difficulty in displacing either of the Balmer brothers but went on to find notoriety as part of our first FA Cup-winning side. Jack Sharp joked that Crelley was an advocate of blood-sports - a snarling predator who loved to chase the ball and who sometimes liked to hunt the man as well. The full-back learned to channel his raw aggression while retaining his reputation for igniting the crowd with his scything tackles.   ★★   Gordon Watson

International appearances
during Everton career

England: 1 cap

Pedigree

South Shields
Sunderland
Everton
Port Vale

**Born: 1897
South Shields**

Blue Stats

	apps	goals
League	290	1
FA Cup	16	0
Other	2	0
Total	308	1
1926/27-35/36		

Warney Cresswell was the 'Prince of Full-Backs' and his reputation for calm assurance has been undimmed by the passage of time. He was signed to aid the white-knuckle spat with relegation in 1927 and helped guarantee survival and provide the impetus for snatching the League crown the next season. Warney took me under his wing and always offered advice: *"Be patient. Master the ball before stroking it to your outside-left."* I remembered his words on my debut at Brentford and, by coincidence, Jackie Coulter scored. Warney served in the forces during both wars but never mentioned that he'd been detained as a prisoner of war. ★★★★★ **Gordon Watson**

Pedigree

Stalybridge Celtic
Stockport County
Everton
Preston North End

Born: 1903
Stockport

Blue Stats

	apps	goals
League	217	37
FA Cup	12	5
Other	1	0
Total	230	42
1926/27-33/34		

Ted Critchley was a rough prototype of David Beckham. He played wide-right and his job was to carpet bomb the box with metronomic accuracy - nothing else was expected of him. I recall that Ted would spend countless lonely hours after training practising his technique. It paid dividends and he developed into a vital part of the teams which earned two League titles between the wars. Cruelly, the flankman was denied the chance to play at Wembley after starring in the semi-final. He was a little bitter and brooded on the side-lines. It was totally out of character and, in a fit of pique, Ted made a beeline for Deepdale. ★★★ **Gordon Watson**

Mr Cuff was Mr Everton. He was our guiding light for over half-a-century and masterminded four championship wins. Mr Cuff ruled the boardroom with an iron fist and didn't suffer fools gladly. He was the most influential administrator in English football and Bill Dean always tugged his forelock before referring to him as 'The Master'. Not surprisingly, only the best was good enough for him. Mr Cuff decreed that only stylish footballers play for Everton and that the kick-and-rush types were not welcome at his School of Science. I hope that the club build a monument to him. Maybe we already have - it's called Goodison Park. ★★★★★ **Gordon Watson**

Pedigree

Adlington
Everton
Rochdale

**Born: 1912
Blackrod**

Blue Stats

	apps	goals
League	174	73
FA Cup	13	3
Other	6	2
Total	193	78

1932/33-43/44

'Nat' Cunliffe's rise from the amateur ranks to international honours was against the odds. He was plucked from the obscurity of the West Lancashire League as a short-term replacement for the injured Bill Dean. 'Nat' brandished exceptional ball control and packed a powerful shot in both feet. But more important, he was driven by a strong will to succeed. Having worked as an apprentice on the railways, he seized his golden opportunity with a vengeance. After Bill's recovery, 'Nat' was moved to inside forward at the expense of Jimmy Dunn. I can vividly picture his pride at earning his one and only England cap in 1936. ★★ **Gordon Watson**

Blue Stats

	apps	goals
League	28/2	2
FA Cup	2	0
Other	4	1
Total	34/2	3
1998/99		

Olivier Dacourt was a riddle, wrapped in mystery, inside an enigma. He was signed to shake the club from its slumbers and, even though he didn't succeed, I'd say that he was our most effective midfield general since the days of Peter Reid. But to be honest, we never saw the very best of him - in fact, we never saw that much of him because of suspensions. In an age of over-fussy refereeing, his combative approach meant that he constantly walked a disciplinary tight-rope. Dacourt picked up a deck of one red and 11 yellow cards in his one season with us. At least we made a few bob from his sojourn by the Mersey. ★★★ **Gordon Watson**

Pedigree

Everton
Wrexham
Tulsa Roughnecks

Born: 1950
Liverpool

Blue Stats

	apps	goals
League	138/10	0
FA Cup	12	0
Other	16/1	0
Total	166/11	0

1967/68-78/79

Terry Darracott wasn't my kind of footballer but he was definitely my kind of Blue. He burst onto the scene as a raw midfield enforcer towards the end of 'The Holy Trinity' era and it took a little time for the fans to warm to him. Of course, it didn't help that he was one of the few local boys in a star-studded line-up. Terry would've played anywhere for Everton and was subsequently converted into an uncompromising full-back. Although his ball distribution was sometimes lax, no-one ever voiced misgivings about his courage or commitment. Terry is also an accomplished coach. In both capacities, he earned his corn every single day.   ★ **Gordon Watson**

International appearances
during Everton career

England: 16 caps

Pedigree

Tranmere Rovers
Everton
Notts County
Sligo Rovers

**Born: 1907
Birkenhead**

Blue Stats

	apps	goals
League	399	349
FA Cup	32	28
Other	2	6
Total	433	383
1924/25-37/38		

I haven't the slightest hesitation in declaring that no-one could hold a candle to Bill Dean - the greatest centre-forward and the greatest goal-scorer of all time. Everyone on Merseyside loved him, irrespective of their persuasion, and Bill made the club famous worldwide. Of course, I'd been raised on stories of his early accomplishments and while I'm not sure that they were all true, I love the idea of him heading a hat-trick after downing a pre-game hat-trick in The Winslow. But I can confirm that some of the goals that Bill scored were out of this world. It was fitting that he died at Goodison - where his spirit lives on. ★★★★★ **Gordon Watson**

William Ralph Dean

International appearances
during Everton career

England: 1 cap

Pedigree

Bolton Wanderers
Burnley
Everton
Burnley
Bury

Born: 1948
Blackburn

Blue Stats

	apps	goals
League	190	29
FA Cup	13	2
Other	27	9
Total	230	40
1974/75-78/79		

Martin Dobson cost a king's ransom in the 1970s and was touted as the best thing since sliced bread. However, the footballing virtuoso was unable to raise the tempo in key games at Everton. Undisputedly, Dobson had all the talents to unlock defences and create goals yet struggled to turn his immense potential into meaningful accomplishment. Some fans groaned that he was more style than content. More likely, he lacked a bit of confidence. My gut instinct was that the only person who never believed in Martin Dobson was 'Dobbo' himself. It was with some embarrassment that he was returned to Turf Moor a little stale.   ★ **Gordon Watson**

Martin Dobson

Pedigree

Sheffield United
Blackpool
Everton
Lincoln City

Born: 1915
Grangemouth

Blue Stats

	apps	goals
League	55	36
FA Cup	3	1
Other	0	0
Total	58	37
1947/48-48/49		

It was difficult for me to get excited about 'Jock' Dodds who was signed to fill the slot vacated by Tommy Lawton. The raging bull cut an impressive figure in the Number 9 shirt, if you ignored the steam belching out of his nostrils, and the mere mention of his name struck fear into most defenders. The Goodison faithful had never witnessed anything like his head-down-and-run approach - and weren't overly impressed. Undaunted, 'Jock' went boldly about his business of snapping up the half-chances that otherwise would've gone begging. I didn't have much in common with him except that his final game was also my last hurrah.   ★ **Gordon Watson**

Ephraim Dodds

International appearances
during Everton career

Eire: 5 caps

Pedigree

Dalymount Rovers
Everton
Grimsby Town

Born: 1929
Cork

Blue Stats

	apps	goals
League	179	2
FA Cup	8	0
Other	0	0
Total	187	2
1951/52-57/58		

Don Donovan arrived at Goodison under somewhat unusual circumstances. Theo Kelly loved to brag that he discovered him during a close-season tour of Ireland when some of the club's hierarchy took an evening stroll and ended up watching an amateur game. Don apparently stood out like a goat in a flock of sheep. He was a commanding player with a temperament well suited to big-time football. Don made meteoric progress and eventually captained the club. I fondly remember his facial expression after scoring his first-ever goal when we thrashed the Busby Babes 5-2 at Old Trafford. He looked traumatised by his luck.   ★★ **Gordon Watson**

Pedigree

Everton

Born: 1857
Liverpool

Blue Stats

	apps	goals
League	0	0
FA Cup	0	0
Other	5	0
Total	5	0
1879/80-84/85		

John Douglas was an enthusiastic pioneer who played cricket and football for St Domingo's. The line-up for our first match at Stanley Park in late 1879 was never recorded, however Douglas is known to have taken part in our second match four weeks later. It ended in another emphatic win over St Peter's. Will Cuff waxed lyrically about Douglas and recalled that he was a casualty of the club's ambitious plan to attract the best players from local rivals. The winger willingly made way for youngsters more adept at the passing-game and was limited to a handful of senior appearances before concentrating on captaining the second-team.   ★★ **Gordon Watson**

International appearances during Everton career

 England: 1 cap

Pedigree

Crook Town
Shildon Athletic
Barnsley
Everton
Brighton & Hove Albion

Born: 1886
Middridge

Blue Stats

	apps	goals
League	92	0
FA Cup	5	0
Other	0	0
Total	97	0
1919/20-23/24		

John Thomas Downs was known as 'The India Rubber Man'. Despite his heavily muscled legs, he was a tremendously agile defender famed for his extravagant overhead clearances. In addition, he is credited with inventing the sliding tackle - a technique subsequently hallmarked by Alex Parker. 'Dickie' was another of my boyhood heroes and, even though he'd gained respect as a firm rock in the sea of troubles which engulfed Goodison in the early-1920s, I've been told that there were gasps of astonishment, shock and horror when he was called up by England. 'Dickie' was awarded his solitary cap at age 35. ★ **Gordon Watson**

Blue Stats

	apps	goals
League	42	0
FA Cup	3	1
Other	0	0
Total	45	1
1889/90-90/91		

Dan Doyle was the most sought-after full-back of his time. The man-mountain could kick the ball an extraordinary distance with pin-point accuracy and, equally as important, could charm the birds from the trees. Doyle crowed about being on the books of Everton and two other clubs at the same time, receiving signing-on bonuses from all three. For a handsome commission, Doyle used his powers of persuasion to entice several other Scottish stars to Everton. After playing a valiant role in capturing the League crown in 1891, Doyle back-tracked to Scotland where he won four more titles with Celtic and also represented his country. ★★★★ **Gordon Watson**

Pedigree

Everton
Wrexham

Born: 1932
Liverpool

Blue Stats

	apps	goals
League	211	0
FA Cup	15	0
Other	5	0
Total	231	0
1956/57-62/63		

Albert Dunlop's cat-like reflexes couldn't compensate for the fact that he was too short for the big League. To everyone's surprise, he beat off competition from Harry Leyland and Jimmy O'Neill to become our first-choice keeper for six seasons, that is until Gordon West showed up. Even then Albert stole the glory during the 1963 championship run-in. If the final game of that season against Fulham was the pinnacle of his career then the 10-4 humiliation at Tottenham in 1958 was the low. I recall that he was a colourful character. Albert was known as 'The Bandit' to his mates and was no stranger to the local constabulary. ★ **Gordon Watson**

International appearances
during Everton career

Scotland: 1 cap

Pedigree

Hibernian
Everton
Exeter City
Runcorn

**Born: 1900
Glasgow**

Blue Stats

	apps	goals
League	140	42
FA Cup	14	7
Other	1	0
Total	155	49
1928/29-34/35		

Jimmy Dunn was a Wembley wizard for both Everton and Scotland. He joined us in 1928 shortly after his success as a member of the famous tartan forward-line that tamed 'The Three Lions' by 5-1. At Everton, the tiny inside-forward continued to torture English defenders with his invention and, for a time, proved to be the perfect foil for Bill Dean. In spite of wearing shin-pads as thick as telephone directories, 'Ginger' was quite nimble and managed to grab his share of important goals as the club claimed three trophies in the early-1930s. None was better than his header against Manchester City in the 1933 FA Cup final. ★★ **Gordon Watson**

Jimmy Dunn

Blue Stats

	apps	goals
League	207/10	13
FA Cup	20	3
Other	20	2
Total	247/10	18

1988/89-96/97

John Ebbrell was a high-profile product of the FA School of Excellence who strove to graduate with honours from the Goodison School of Science. Even though he captained the England Under-21 team, his efforts were never fully appreciated by toffee nose-in-the-air purists. Maybe too much was expected of him. I liked Ebbrell. He could tackle with venom, pass with precision and had a good engine. His progress was dogged by injuries. In many ways he was a victim of his own courage and attempts to cheat pain. Ebbrell never got the rub of the green and should have been included in the 1995 Cup final squad. ★★ Gordon Watson

International appearances
during Everton career

 Northern Ireland
& Eire: 28 caps

Pedigree

Shamrock Rovers
Everton
Tranmere Rovers

**Born: 1923
Dublin**

Blue Stats

	apps	goals
League	394	76
FA Cup	34	6
Other	0	0
Total	428	82
1946/47-56/57		

Tommy Eglington was an exciting winger with a Kanchelskis-type change of pace. Tommy had the fastest feet in the game and Theo Kelly often joked that he'd received a complaint from fans in the Paddock about the smell of scorched turf. I recall that the kids in the Boys' Pen christened him 'Flash'. He was also a lethal finisher and scored five times in one game against Doncaster. He was capped by both Eire and Northern Ireland and, in addition, holds the dubious distinction of having featured in more Division Two games than any other Everton player. Tommy was a loyal club-man and still travels from Dublin to our home fixtures. ★★★★ **Gordon Watson**

Pedigree

Everton

Born: 1868
Dublin

Blue Stats

	apps	goals
League	14	1
FA Cup	1	0
Other	0	0
Total	15	1

1891/92-95/96

Jack Elliott displayed a near-religious devotion to Everton. Before the turn-of-the-century, he'd been a forward who lacked a yard of pace and, as a result, was unable to hold down a regular first-team place. Elliott was always ready and willing to turn out in emergencies and also worked hard at developing the club's up-and-coming talent. Eventually, he was appointed chief trainer and became an important part of the Goodison set-up. I've noticed that he was included on every team-photograph for 20 years or so. Today, when money is worshiped at a higher altar than legends, football clubs still need men like him.   ★★ Gordon Watson

Pedigree

Oswestry
Everton

Born: 1860
Oswestry

Blue Stats

	apps	goals
League	31	1
FA Cup	0	0
Other	133	70
Total	164	71
1884/85-89/90		

George Farmer was one of our first legitimate professionals. He was paid thirty bob a week, about double a working-man's wage in 1885. Of course, boot-money had been common practice but was strenuously denied by the leading clubs in the North West. And with the benefit of big crowds, Everton could afford to embrace professionalism. Consequently, Farmer was able to devote more of his time to football and flourished as an exciting forward. The record books show that he scored our first goal in the FA Cup but his real claim to fame was as a provider. Farmer set up both goals for George Fleming in our first League fixture. ★ **Gordon Watson**

International appearances
during Everton career

 Northern Ireland
& Eire: 33 caps

Pedigree

Shamrock Rovers
Everton
Tranmere Rovers
Holyhead
Shamrock Rovers

**Born: 1922
Dublin**

Blue Stats

	apps	goals
League	422	13
FA Cup	31	4
Other	0	0
Total	453	17
1946/47-56/57		

Peter Farrell was a spirited leader, a gentleman footballer and a true Blue. Signed by Theo Kelly as a cheap replacement for Joe Mercer, he matured into a tough but honest competitor who tackled with conviction and wore his royal blue colours with immense pride. I played alongside him for a while and was impressed by his encouragement to all of his team-mates - both young and old. Peter had an unassuming manner off the pitch, perhaps it had something to do with his smouldering briar, and never once mentioned that he had captained the first foreign side to win in England. Or that he had scored in that game. ★★★★★ Gordon Watson

International appearances
during Everton career

♛ Eire: 4 caps

Pedigree

Home Farm
Aston Villa
Rotherham United (loan)
Everton
Bolton Wanderers

Born: 1975
Dublin

Blue Stats

	apps	goals
League	18/9	1
FA Cup	1	0
Other	2	1
Total	21/9	2
1997/98-98/99		

Hero or zero? Gareth Farrelly was the first signing of Howard Kendall's third spell in charge. As a lifelong Blue, he jumped at the opportunity to move to Everton but took some time to settle. Quite often the mid-fielder drifted ineffectively round the park and, not surprisingly, received a chorus of tongue lashings from his detractors as we clung to our Premiership status. But cometh the moment, cometh the Irishman. And it was Farrelly of all people who kept us in the big league by scoring an absolute gem against Coventry City. Needless to say, his goal sent Goodison delirious. God bless you - Gareth Farrelly. Thank you - St Jude. ★ **Gordon Watson**

Pedigree

Lincoln City
Everton
Port Vale

Born: 1890
Measham

Blue Stats

	apps	goals
League	219	0
FA Cup	12	0
Other	40	0
Total	271	0
1913/14-23/24		

Tom Fern filled the gap between the sticks created by Billy Scott's surprise exit. It was no small task but he was equal to the job. Fern was an athletic keeper with something of an uncharitable disposition who was quite capable of looking after himself when confronted by robust forwards. His harmony with both Jimmy Galt and Tom Fleetwood resulted in a near-impregnable rearguard as we strolled to the Division One title in 1915. Will Cuff strongly believed that if Fern had played in the semi-final against Chelsea then we'd have won the double that season. His career bridged World War I but never reached the same standards afterwards.   ★★ **Gordon Watson**

Pedigree

Charlton Athletic
Walthamstowe Avenue
Everton
Southport

Born: 1919
London

Blue Stats

	apps	goals
League	380	49
FA Cup	30	5
Other	0	0
Total	410	54
1945/46-58/59		

Wally Fielding was a brilliant schemer and ran our engine-room for more than a decade. Admired for his effervescent enthusiasm as much as for his flawless distribution, the inside-left was amazingly all right foot. In addition, 'Nobby' was conspicuous on the pitch as an emaciated symbol of the post-war period. I'd seen more meat in a Sayer's pasty. Nevertheless, the little fellow could master most challenges. The only time that I saw 'Nobby' in any real difficulty was during the brief reign of Ian Buchan when he had to take part in a gruelling weight-lifting programme. He buckled under the strain of the empty bar. ★★★★ **Gordon Watson**

Pedigree

Bolton Wanderers
Hindley Central
Rochdale
Everton
Oldham Athletic

**Born: 1888
Kirkby**

Blue Stats

	apps	goals
League	264	9
FA Cup	21	1
Other	121	11
Total	406	21
1910/11-22/23		

Tom Fleetwood was a dyed-in-the-wool Blue whose unflinching contributions have been almost neglected by most historians. He was discovered playing non-League football and developed into a mainstay in the Goodison set-up for a dozen years or more. Forceful on the ground and no slouch in the air, Fleetwood occupied the right-half slot throughout the 1915 championship campaign and later turned out at centre-half. He represented England in two unofficial Victory internationals but was never capped. Will Cuff declared that Tom Fleetwood could have walked over molten lava for Everton - without getting blisters. ★★★ **Gordon Watson**

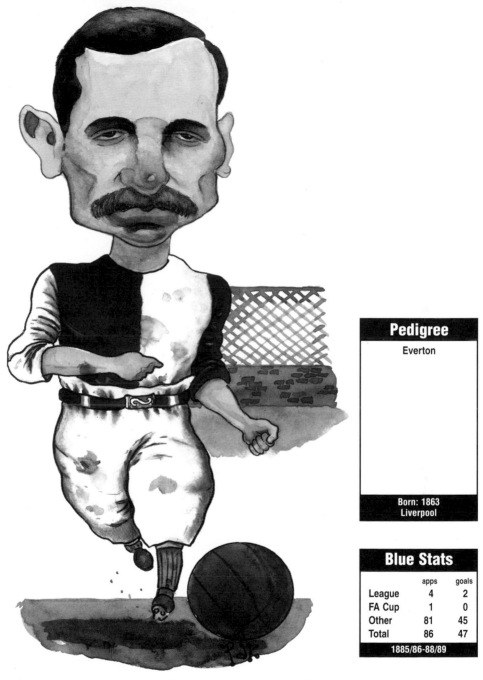

Pedigree

Everton

Born: 1863
Liverpool

Blue Stats

	apps	goals
League	4	2
FA Cup	1	0
Other	81	45
Total	86	47

1885/86-88/89

George Fleming was an amateur jack-of-all-trades who enjoyed three seasons in the first-team prior to the formation of the Football League. Fleming loved to flaunt his superior dribbling skills and also needed no invitation to unleash his powerful shot. He had featured in the sides that won the Liverpool Cup in 1886 and 1887 before securing his place in the club's annals by scoring twice in our first League game. Both goals were clinical finishes. The opener came from a header, the second from a half-volley. Fleming left his stud marks in history and ghosted away. Nobody seems to know what became of him.

★ **Gordon Watson**

George Fleming **83**

International appearances
during Everton career

 England: 2 caps

Pedigree

Aston Villa
Woolwich Arsenal
Everton
Burnley
Wigan Borough
Kettering Town

Born: 1885
Birmingham

Blue Stats

	apps	goals
League	86	63
FA Cup	8	4
Other	0	0
Total	94	67
1907/08-10/11		

Without question, Bertie Freeman lived up to his star billing. He was a real fox-in-the-box and his uncanny knack for tucking away half-chances with either foot enabled him to net 38 times in 37 League games during the 1908/09 season. Unfortunately, that campaign ended with much wailing and gnashing of teeth as we finished runners-up to Newcastle United. Nevertheless, Freeman's record haul remained unsurpassed until eclipsed by Bill Dean nearly two decades later. Will Cuff believed that the club had been too hasty in selling him to Burnley where he was the League's top marksman again in 1912 and 1913.

★★★★★ **Gordon Watson**

International appearances
during Everton career

 Scotland: 2 caps

Pedigree

Dundee North End
Dundee
Everton
Southampton
Bournemouth
Swindon Town
Brentford
Seattle Sounders

**Born: 1940
Dundee**

Blue Stats

	apps	goals
League	255/1	33
FA Cup	25	2
Other	23	2
Total	303/1	37
1959/60-66/67		

Jimmy Gabriel may have lacked the touch of an angel but was blessed with a devout passion for football. The powerful right-half was heralded as the new Dave Mackay and could turn defence into attack with his penetrating forays. 'Gabby' was as strong as an ox. He wore his royal blue heart on his sleeve both on and off the park and inspired his colleagues. With his name on the team-sheet, the sun seemed to rise with an Everton toffee in its mouth. He returned to Goodison and joined the coaching staff in 1987. 'Gabby' was also brave enough to pick up the poisoned chalice as caretaker-manager on two occasions. ★★★★ **Gordon Watson**

Pedigree

Ardeer Thistle
Rangers
Everton
Third Lanark

Born: 1885
Saltcoats

Blue Stats

	apps	goals
League	32	2
FA Cup	4	2
Other	0	0
Total	36	4
1914/15		

Jimmy Galt confirmed that successful sides are built from the back by organising a steel blanket of denial in front of the goal. Although the Scotland international was a little long in the tooth, his iron lungs and his granite tackle transformed our fortunes overnight. Galt strained every nerve and every sinew for Everton and was widely regarded as the most hard-working player in the 1915 championship side. Sadly, World War I restricted him to only one season at Goodison and his involvement in English football was over before it had barely started. I've learned that Galt was severely shell-shocked during that war.

★★★ Gordon Watson

International appearances
during Everton career

England: 2 caps

Pedigree

Notts County
Notts Rangers
Grimsby Town
Everton
Liverpool

Born: 1868
Nottingham

Blue Stats

	apps	goals
League	91	78
FA Cup	7	8
Other	0	0
Total	98	86
1889/90-94/95		

'Goal-a-game' Geary made up for his physical limitations with turbo-charged bursts of speed which terrified defences. Also his cunning and sharpness in and around the penalty area made him one of the great goal-poachers of the nineteenth century. He spearheaded the team which won the League title for the first time and finished runners-up on two other occasions. Geary was recognised as Everton's pin-up boy until the signing of Jack Southworth resulted in him defecting to Liverpool in 1895. By then, he'd already secured his place in our history - as the first Everton player to score at Goodison Park. ★★★★★ **Gordon Watson**

Fred Geary 87

International appearances
during Everton career

England: 3 caps

Pedigree

Reddish Green Wesleyans
Stockport County
Everton

**Born: 1909
Stockport**

Blue Stats

	apps	goals
League	196	2
FA Cup	15	0
Other	4	0
Total	215	2
1930/31-39/40		

Charlie Gee was another of Will Cuff's discoveries who made the unbelievable rise from anonymity to international stardom. The young centre-half was still wet behind the ears when he arrived at Goodison but was playing for England within 12 months. Charlie was a good all-round performer blessed with a shrewd understanding of the game. I learned a lot from him. He made defending look easy and his composure underpinned the club's push for promotion in 1931 and the Division 1 title the following season. Few people know that Charlie insisted that Everton take a look at a little known forward named Harry Catterick. ★★★★ **Gordon Watson**

International appearances
during Everton career

England: 4 caps

Pedigree

Bradford Park Avenue
Everton
Bolton Wanderers
Darwen

Born: 1914
Bradford

Blue Stats

	apps	goals
League	167	31
FA Cup	12	6
Other	2	0
Total	181	37
1932/33-37/38		

Albert Geldard had been the youngest player to appear in a League game when he debuted for the Bradford Park Avenue in 1929. By the time he'd signed for Everton, Albert had evolved into one of the fastest wingers of all time. He was quick enough to catch pigeons but I remember that defenders were more terrified by his devastating acceleration. Albert exploded past them. Of course, he was more than a speed-merchant and his magical ball skills also enabled him to wriggle his way through defences. Albert was an accomplished conjuror both on and off the pitch and was still in his prime when he was allowed to join Bolton. ★★★★ **Gordon Watson**

Pedigree

Aston Villa
Everton
Manchester United
Manchester City
Stoke City
Darlington

Born: 1954
Liverpool

Blue Stats

	apps	goals
League	64	2
FA Cup	11	0
Other	3	1
Total	78	3
1979/80-80/81		

John Gidman loved to embark on marauding overlaps and create something out of nothing. The England full-back was signed by Gordon Lee for a record fee and was reckoned by many to be the best in the land. I thought that he looked like a very classy acquisition until his progress was plagued by injuries. With the rapid development of Gary Stevens and Brian Borrows, he was off-loaded to Old Trafford in the deal which landed us with Mickey Thomas for a stormy few months. No doubt Gidman had the last laugh by starring in two cup final triumphs over Everton, for Aston Villa in 1977 and for Manchester United in 1985.   ★★ **Gordon Watson**

International appearances
during Everton career

Scotland: 5 caps

Pedigree

Petershill
Rangers
Everton
Rangers
Partick Thistle

Born: 1915
Airdrie

Blue Stats

	apps	goals
League	121	40
FA Cup	12	4
Other	7	3
Total	140	47
1935/36-39/40		

Torry Gillick was an outrageous crowd-pleaser. The outside-right was tremendously gifted and his sublime footwork set up a bonanza of goals during our 1939 championship triumph. He was always surrounded by breathless admirers - his team-mates. I used to stop and marvel at him. He was that good. Torry had the world at his feet but was denied further success by the outbreak of World War II. He was my best mate and I was deeply saddened by his decision to go back to Ibrox, where he subsequently won League, Cup and League Cup medals. Torry was the top Scottish winger of his day and possibly any other day. ★★★★★ **Gordon Watson**

Pedigree

Everton
Fulham
NAC Breda
Den Haag
Scunthorpe United
South China
Tranmere Rovers
Barrow

Born: 1953
Liverpool

Blue Stats

	apps	goals
League	31/4	2
FA Cup	7	0
Other	9	0
Total	47/4	2
1975/76-77/78		

Ronnie Goodlass was a genuine blue-boy who won the admiration of Gwladys Street. With all due respect to Duncan McKenzie, in my view, it was Goodlass who was magic in the Seventies. He had to overcome special challenges but always wore his blue and white with genuine pride. Goodlass added beautiful balance to his seductive sorcery and excelled at one-on-one confrontations. He'd roast his markers before reaching the by-line and crossing with laser accuracy. I recall that no-one could get near him during both cup runs in 1977. His career sizzled then fizzled out after Dave Thomas appeared on the horizon. ★★ **Gordon Watson**

Pedigree

High Spen Athletic
Everton
Rochdale
Southport

Born: 1924
High Spen

Blue Stats

	apps	goals
League	121	10
FA Cup	12	1
Other	92	6
Total	225	17
1942/43-54/55		

Jackie Grant was a battling wing-half. I played around 100 games with him in war-time football and knew him to be firm in the tackle and capable of delivering probing passes. But I was most impressed by the little fellow's big heart. He had to vie with Stan Bentham and Peter Farrell for the vacancy created by Joe Mercer's departure and became a first-team regular in the side demoted in 1951. Though the writing was on the wall for Everton, having scored only two goals in the final 11 games, Jackie was absolutely inconsolable after the 6-0 thrashing at Sheffield Wednesday sent us down. It was worse than a death in the family.   ★ **Gordon Watson**

International appearances
during Everton career

 Scotland: 1 cap

Pedigree

Dundee United
Aston Villa
Wolverhampton Wanderers
Everton
Aston Villa
Notts County
West Bromwich Albion
Rangers
Cheltenham Town

Born: 1955
Glasgow

Blue Stats

	apps	goals
League	44/5	14
FA Cup	14/1	3
Other	3/1	5
Total	61/7	22
1983/84-84/85		

Andy Gray was sent to Goodison from heaven. Only six years after being voted Players' Player of the Year and Young Player of the Year, the bravest striker of his day was rescued from the scrap-heap by Howard Kendall. In return, Gray led the Everton line with gusto and opponents were guaranteed to come away with more than a few lumps and bumps. He was an exhilarating sight when in full flight and also scored his share of goals. His two headers against Sunderland in 1985 were out of this world. Many of his team-mates have told me that it was Gray's charisma rather than his goals which helped to turn the club around. ★★★★ **Gordon Watson**

Pedigree

Bolton Wanderers
New Brighton
Everton
Bangor City

**Born: 1914
Bolton**

Blue Stats

	apps	goals
League	106	1
FA Cup	9	0
Other	223	2
Total	338	3
1937/38-48/49		

Norman Greenhalgh was a down-to-earth Lancashire lad. Known as 'Rollicker' behind his back, the defender was revered in a world of genuinely tough characters. Norman worked at improving his technique and fostered a frightful union with Billy Cook. They would boot wingers up in the air and prided themselves on waiting until their victims had landed before kicking them again. Few wingers broke free of their shackles and Stan Matthews claimed that he hated to play against Norman. He was the team-mate that I least enjoyed facing in training but showed his true mettle as the only ever-present in our championship side. ★★★ **Gordon Watson**

Pedigree

North Shields Athletic
Everton
South Shields

Born: 1892
North Shields

Blue Stats

	apps	goals
League	142	9
FA Cup	6	0
Other	119	9
Total	267	18
1910/11-22/23		

Alan Grenyer's manner was both forceful and fluid. Nurtured as a long-term replacement for Harry Makepeace, he learned well at his master's knee and progressed by leaps and bounds to contest the left-half slot with his mentor prior to the outbreak of World War I. Harry Cooke told me that Grenyer had the benefits of youth - extra zip in his stride and extra snap in the tackle. He made enough appearances to earn a championship medal in 1915 and was also picked to play for England in a Victory international. Inexplicably, Grenyer struggled to scale anything like the heights expected of him after the hostilities had ceased.   ★ **Gordon Watson**

International appearances
during Everton career

♛ Wales: 8 caps

Pedigree

Wrexham
Everton
Bolton Wanderers
Middlesbrough
Aston Villa

Born: 1905
Wrexham

Blue Stats

	apps	goals
League	76	9
FA Cup	2	0
Other	0	0
Total	78	9
1926/27-30/31		

Tom Griffiths never claimed to be the daintiest of centre-halves. He was recruited from Wrexham and was Welsh to the core - but was no TG Jones. In fact they were from different footballing worlds. Griffiths was a throwback to the no-nonsense pivot who was fearless and rugged. He was seldom beaten in the air but less imposing on the deck where he treated the ball like a hot potato. Griffiths prided himself on rarely being caught in possession and always opted to dispatch long clearances, sometimes finding men in blue. His claim to fame - he was part of our first side to be relegated as well as our first side to be promoted.

★ **Gordon Watson**

International appearances
during Everton career

Northern Ireland: 11 caps

Pedigree

Linfield
Ipswich Town
Everton
Millwall
Swindon Town
Tranmere Rovers

Born: 1946
Belfast

Blue Stats

	apps	goals
League	38/3	5
FA Cup	2/2	0
Other	7/2	0
Total	47/7	5
1975/76-76/77		

Bryan Hamilton was the key witness to the FA Cup crime of the century. The offence: daylight robbery. The date: April 23, 1977. The scene: Maine Road. The victim: Everton Football Club. The culprit: Mr Clive Thomas of Treorchy. The facts: the arrogant ref robbed Hamilton of a late winner in a semi-final clash with Liverpool. And to date, he has shown no remorse. Of course, we've grown used to such injustice. After all, it's not the only time that our neighbours have soiled our doorstep then washed their hands. The midfielder deserves to be remembered for his whole-hearted approach - he was prepared to run until he dropped.　　　★　**Gordon Watson**

Pedigree

Renton
Everton
Renton
Liverpool

**Born: 1864
Renton**

Blue Stats

	apps	goals
League	42	0
FA Cup	2	0
Other	0	0
Total	44	0
1889/90-90/91		

Andrew Hannah was the first Everton captain to lift the championship trophy. He was also the first man to get his hands on the silverware because Preston, the previous winners, had only received Football League flags. The right-back portrayed a fearsome persona and became part of the the bedrock of the side which came second in 1890 and top in 1891. Hannah was well rewarded and was one of football's highest earners at £3 per week. He also holds the distinction of winning the Scottish title with Renton and the stigma of leading Liverpool out of Division Two. In addition, he was the first Blue to compete at the Highland Games. ★★★ **Gordon Watson**

International appearances
during Everton career

 England: 4 caps

Pedigree

Blackpool
Everton
Manchester United
Bradford City
Stoke
Northern Nomads

**Born: 1882
Manchester**

Blue Stats

	apps	goals
League	130	25
FA Cup	26	4
Other	0	0
Total	156	29

1903/04-07/08

Harold Hardman was a gentleman, a scholar and our first Olympic champion. His fine turn of speed and insatiable desire to be in the thick of the action made him a big favourite at Goodison. The winger played in consecutive FA Cup finals and was only one of three amateurs to have won a winners' medal in the twentieth century. But Hardman's top priority was his legal practice which was based in Manchester and, as a consequence, he struggled to find time for serious training at Everton. After some soul-searching, he moved to Old Trafford. I believe that Hardman was a Manchester United director for more than half-a-century. ★★★★ **Gordon Watson**

Pedigree

Liverpool
Everton
Sheffield Wednesday
Manchester City
Everton
Luton Town
Burnley
Cardiff City

Born: 1960
Liverpool

Blue Stats

	apps	goals
League	148/30	4
FA Cup	12/9	1
Other	37/4	0
Total	197/43	5

1983/84-87/88 & 91/92-92/93

Alan Harper was the model for modern utility men. Known as 'Bertie' to his many friends, he was signed by Howard Kendall from Liverpool. Harper repaid the modest transfer fee many times over with stalwart performances and was one of the unsung heroes of our treasure hunt in the 1980s. Harper was well-equipped to fill most defensive and midfield berths but, although he was never tagged 'super-sub', I suspect that substitute was his most productive role. He even came off the bench to score in the 1986 FA Cup semi-final. Harper had two stints at the club as a player and also returned as a youth coach of some eminence.   ★★ **Gordon Watson**

Pedigree

Everton
Cardiff City
Newport County

Born: 1935
Bebington

Blue Stats

	apps	goals
League	310	23
FA Cup	31	4
Other	17	2
Total	358	29
1955/56-66/67		

Brian Harris was an adaptable footballer with no little skill. Although he had to make way for Tony Kay in the 1963 championship team, Harris took the set-back in his stride and his loyalty won a special place in Everton folklore. 'Hooky' was a laugh-a-minute. I remember him appearing on television during our Australian tour in the Sixties. He was so funny that he gave an encore the next night. But perhaps 'Hooky' saved his best performance for the 1966 FA Cup final when he was arguably the man-of-the-match. Who can forget him borrowing the bobby's helmet as Eddy Cavanagh made his debut on the hallowed turf? ★★★ **Gordon Watson**

Pedigree

Everton
Birmingham City
Oldham Athletic

Born: 1933
Birkenhead

Blue Stats

	apps	goals
League	191	65
FA Cup	14	5
Other	2	2
Total	207	72
1955/56-60/61		

Jimmy Harris was a dashing forward who pushed Dave Hickson out of the Goodison back-door on two occasions. I recall that he possessed a decent touch and a tremendous shot. More than anything, Jimmy had searing pace. He ran like a hungry cheetah leaving defenders to taste his dust. On good days Jimmy resembled Gary Lineker, on others he was like Stuart Barlow. He also scored lots of goals including a hat-trick at White Hart Lane when we were thumped 10-4. Just like Frank Wignall, another very promising forward, Jimmy was unfortunate to be around at the same time as Mr Moores' cheque book.

★ **Gordon Watson**

Jimmy Harris

Pedigree

Shelbourne
Everton
Shelbourne

**Born: 1885
Dublin**

Blue Stats

	apps	goals
League	190	1
FA Cup	24	1
Other	0	0
Total	214	2
1907/08-13/14		

Val Harris arrived at Goodison accompanied by much pomp and ceremony. He was trumpeted as the superstar of the Emerald Isle - an early fore-runner of the much-maligned Martin Murray. Harris experienced no difficulty in living up to his reputation and choreographed performances of passing and movement. In addition to his impressive portfolio of silky skills, the right-half owned a fiery nature. He had a wild glint in his eye and was often involved in confrontations. Despite his stalwart battles, we won no major honours during his rousing spell at Everton. Perhaps more than anything, Harris lacked the luck of the Irish. ★★ **Gordon Watson**

International appearances
during Everton career

♛ England: 2 caps

Pedigree

Gresley Rovers
Leicester City
Everton
Preston North End
Blackpool

**Born: 1891
Church Gresley**

Blue Stats

	apps	goals
League	177	17
FA Cup	13	0
Other	47	10
Total	237	27
1913/14-23/24		

'Jud' Harrison was an explosive player with a shot like a NASA rocket. The stocky left-winger boasted the hardest shot in the country and, in the days before radar, it was claimed that the ball hit the back of the net at around 80 miles per hour. The ferocity may have been exaggerated but Ted Sagar divulged to me that his firepower must have been awesome because keeper Tom Fern refused to face him in training. Allegedly, one of Harrison's rockets had snapped a wooden crossbar. He was also admired for his unstinting service as Bobby Parker and Joe Clennell ran riot throughout the 1915 championship crusade.　★★　Gordon Watson

George Harrison　　105

Pedigree

Airdrieonians
Everton

Born: 1897
Glasgow

Blue Stats

	apps	goals
League	289	5
FA Cup	11	0
Other	1	0
Total	301	5

1921/22-29/30

Hunter Hart was a real hero - 'The Admiral Nelson of Goodison'. He never allowed his handicap, the loss of an eye in a childhood accident, to undermine his career. Hunter was a never-say-die defender who tackled with courage and determination and distributed the ball with patience and precision. He engineered a couple of relegation escapes before captaining our push for the title in 1927. Inexplicably, we finished at the bottom of the table a few years later. Division Two wasn't the end of the world but many Blues could see it from there. Consequently, Hunter retired to work alongside Tom McIntosh as assistant-secretary. ★★★★ Gordon Watson

International appearances
during Everton career

Scotland: 7 caps

Pedigree

West Bromwich Albion
Manchester City
Everton
Nottingham Forest
Manchester City
Fort Lauderdale Strikers
Norwich City
Bolton Wanderers
Stockport County
Oldham Athletic
Shrewsbury Town

Born: 1950
Clydebank

Blue Stats

	apps	goals
League	81	6
FA Cup	11	1
Other	6	0
Total	98	7
1979/80-81/82		

Asa Hartford was blessed with every prerequisite for success at the top. Signed by Gordon Lee in 1979, the midfield dynamo was welcomed as the saviour that we'd been waiting for. Alas, he was no Messiah but his all-action approach shook Goodison. He certainly converted me. Hartford was a buzz-bomb whose zest for the game inspired his team-mates. Although damned with a hole-in-the-heart condition and rejected by several major clubs, he had a tremendous engine. Indeed, Hartford ran his socks off week-in and week-out but I think that he was more effective in the blue shirts of Manchester City and Scotland. ★★★★ **Gordon Watson**

International appearances
during Everton career

♛ England: 1 cap

Pedigree

Everton
Sheffield Wednesday

Born: 1944
Liverpool

Blue Stats

	apps	goals
League	317/4	18
FA Cup	34	4
Other	31/1	2
Total	382/5	24
1963/64-74/75		

Colin Harvey was the most complete player to have turned out for Everton in the post-war era. He was our own George Best without the distractions of dollybirds and Lotus Europas. 'Charlie' combined the qualities of an elegant footballer with those of an awesome athlete. The fans didn't call him 'The White Pelé' for nothing. He displayed immaculate ball control, imaginative passing, valiant tackling, prodigious running and much more. As a player, he was the cream of 'The Holy Trinity' of Kendall, Harvey & Ball. As a coach, he made tremendous inputs to our success in the Eighties. But as a boss, he was merely human. ★★★★★ **Gordon Watson**

Pedigree

Stoke City
Everton
Espanyol
Aston Villa
Manchester City
Stoke City
Burnley
Sheffield United

Born: 1961
Stoke on Trent

Blue Stats

	apps	goals
League	206/20	71
FA Cup	24/5	6
Other	50/3	17
Total	280/28	94
1981/82-88/89		

Adrian Heath's sharpness enabled him to be deployed as an out-and-out striker, hover behind the front-men or forage in midfield. 'Inchy' etched his place in our history by intercepting Kevin Brock's back-pass to snatch an equaliser in a Milk Cup tie at Oxford and inspiring our progress to two Wembley finals in 1984. However, my lasting impression is his extra-time winner in the semi-final at Highbury - when he soared above the Southampton defence to glide a header past Peter Shilton. He would've made an even greater impact and gained England caps had he not been crudely hospitalised by Sheffield Wednesday's Brian Marwood.   ★★★ **Gordon Watson**

Adrian Heath   109

Pedigree

Ellesmere Port Town
Everton
Aston Villa
Huddersfield Town
Everton
Liverpool
Cambridge United
Bury
Tranmere Rovers
Ballymena United

Born: 1929
Salford

Blue Stats

	apps	goals
League	225	95
FA Cup	18	16
Other	0	0
Total	243	111

1951/52-55/56 & 57/58-59/60

Dave Hickson was widely known as 'The Cannonball Kid'. He was an old-fashioned Andy Gray - a swashbuckling Number 9 who displayed superior heading skills and immense courage. Unassuming off the field, Dave became a gladiator when attired in royal blue. He seemed to be always covered in blood - not always his own - and some of us thought that he was a bit crazy. At times he acted like a rogue elephant - his worst enemy being, of course, himself. Dave had two spells at Goodison and was worshiped by the fans. To be honest, I've never figured out why he did the dirty and relocated his blond quiff to Anfield.   ★★★★ **Gordon Watson**

Pedigree

Everton
Manchester United
Bury
Stoke City

Born: 1958
Buxton

Blue Stats

	apps	goals
League	150/1	6
FA Cup	7	0
Other	22/2	0
Total	179/3	6
1976/77-83/84		

Mark Higgins's career ended in tears. The central defender had been awarded a record number of schoolboy caps and had been tipped for the top by just about everyone in the game. He was very good in the air, very strong in the tackle and very assured on the ball. Higgins also wore the captain's arm-band with integrity. He led by example and, having steered the club through some lean years, was on the verge of an England call-up when crippled by a pelvic condition in late-1983. Higgins was forced into retirement at the tender age of 25 and witnessed our glory years from the stands. The fickle finger of fate was unkind to him. ★★ **Gordon Watson**

Pedigree

United Church
Everton

Born: 1856
Liverpool

Blue Stats

	apps	goals
League	1	0
FA Cup	5	0
Other	152	36
Total	158	36
1880/81-88/89		

Mike Higgins played in the early Everton sides nicknamed 'The Black Watch' and 'The Moonlight Dribblers'. Under the direction of Jack McGill, he abandoned his natural dribbling game for the short-passing approach preferred north of the border. Higgins was an odd-job man and featured in eight different positions. He was a mainstay in the first Everton team to capture a trophy, the Liverpool Cup in 1884. Higgins was also involved in many other firsts - our first game at Priory Road, our first game at Anfield and our first FA Cup tie. He played only one League game but served on the Everton committee for several years. ★★ **Gordon Watson**

International appearances
during Everton career

England: 4 caps

Pedigree

Manchester City
Everton
Sheffield Wednesday

Born: 1969
Manchester

Blue Stats

	apps	goals
League	170/12	7
FA Cup	12/2	1
Other	25/2	1
Total	207/16	9
1990/91-97/98		

Andy Hinchcliffe was the thinking-man's David Beckham of his day who made a small fortune from exploiting his very special talent. He could whip in crosses with intelligence and accuracy. Unkindly, some critics claimed that the left-back cum wing-back also defended like Beckham. Signed by Colin Harvey, he subsequently honed his skill to near-perfection under the guidance of Joe Royle. His set-pieces and crosses punctuated the 1995 FA Cup run and even elevated him to the England side. However with the return of Howard Kendall as Everton manager, Hinchcliffe was soon on his bike to Sheffield Wednesday.

★ **Gordon Watson**

International appearances
during Everton career

England: 9 caps

Pedigree

Church
Bootle
Everton
Reading

Born: 1865
Blackburn

Blue Stats

	apps	goals
League	225	3
FA Cup	27	1
Other	0	0
Total	252	4
1888/89-97/98		

Johnny Holt was the club's first England international. He was signed from arch-rivals Bootle just in time for the inaugural League season. Holt was an authoritative centre-half and, along with Nick Ross and Dan Doyle, was widely regarded as one of the best defenders of the Victorian era. Labelled 'The Little Devil' by all who crossed his path, he excelled at man-marking. Will Cuff said that Holt was tiny, much shorter than his official height of 5 ft 4 in, but rarely came off second best. He was capable of out-jumping taller forwards and his terrier-like persistence, not to mention his sly fouls, often niggled opponents into making errors.   ★★★★★ **Gordon Watson**

International appearances
during Everton career

Wales: 23 caps

Pedigree

Rhyl
Wrexham
Portsmouth
Southampton
Everton
Birmingham City
Huddersfield Town
Kidderminster Harriers
Walsall
Belper Town

**Born: 1962
St Asaph**

Blue Stats

	apps	goals
League	118/5	3
FA Cup	11/1	0
Other	15/1	0
Total	144/7	3
1992/93-95/96		

Barry Horne enjoyed a love affair with Gwladys Street. First, he was one of us. Second, he was a abrasive ball-winner who slogged away in the middle of the park meting out tackles. His blood-and-guts challenges would ignite everyone around him. Famed as a 'Dog of War' who out-fought Manchester United in 1995 to win the FA Cup, Horne will always be celebrated for launching the missile which had helped to save our Premiership status 12 months earlier. I can close my eyes and picture him ploughing through the Wimbledon ranks, as well as the rubble of a relegation nightmare, to earn an unassailable place in our hearts and minds. ★★★ **Gordon Watson**

Pedigree

Everton
Oldham Athletic

Born: 1947
Blackpool

Blue Stats

	apps	goals
League	336/15	29
FA Cup	30/2	4
Other	22/1	1
Total	388/18	34
1965/66-75/76		

John Hurst formed a near-perfect partnership with Brian Labone at the core of our defence for more than 300 games. Even before his introduction as our first-ever substitute in 1965, I was impressed by the old head on his young shoulders and honestly can't remember him putting a foot wrong. John loved to make good use of the ball. He always built constructively from the back and linked up with his star-studded midfield. John earned a bunch of England Under-23 caps but never gained full honours. He was a quiet man who rarely beat his own drum and his aspirations were continually thwarted by the form of Bobby Moore. ★★★★ **Gordon Watson**

Pedigree

Everton
Luton Town
Memphis Rouges

Born: 1947
Newcastle upon Tyne

Blue Stats

	apps	goals
League	158/7	44
FA Cup	22	10
Other	10/1	1
Total	190/8	55
1964/65-73/74		

Jimmy Husband was a product of Harry Catterick's nursery scheme. He was an unpredictable forward who was admired for his lively pace and hypnotic body swerve. When in full flow, 'Skippy' paralysed defences with his scintillating diagonal runs and dovetailed with Joe Royle to form the most exciting young strike-force in the country. Jimmy was very special. No-one knew what he was going to do next and I'm not sure that he did either. Cruelly, his glittering future was halted by a savage tackle from Dave Mackay of Derby which seemed to shatter his verve. Jimmy shrank into his shell and was never quite the same again. ★★★ **Gordon Watson**

♛ Scotland: 8 caps

Pedigree

Hartlepool United
Liverpool
West Ham United
Sheffield United
Everton
Sunderland
West Ham United

**Born: 1971
Gateshead**

Blue Stats

	apps	goals
League	68/7	10
FA Cup	9	0
Other	4/1	1
Total	81/8	11
1997/98-99/00		

Don Hutchison darkened our threshold ladened with some excess baggage. He had acquired a reputation for being something of a reckless boy on the pitch and a silly boy off the pitch and much hullabaloo was associated with his arrival. 'Hutch' relished the challenge and matured into a decent player for both Everton and Scotland. He always gave 100% and made up for his lack of pace with creative passing, combative tackling and a keen eye for the onion bag. The ex-Red never let us down and it's hard to refute that, more often than not, he appeared to be the only member of a rudderless team with any real fire in his belly. ★★ **Gordon Watson**

International appearances
during Everton career

Ireland &
Northern Ireland: 11 caps

Pedigree

Dunmurry
Everton
Portsmouth
Connah's Quay
Derry City

Born: 1899
Lisburn

Blue Stats

	apps	goals
League	199	54
FA Cup	15	3
Other	0	0
Total	214	57

1921/22-27/28

Bobby Irvine concocted goals out of thin air. Discovered in the bowels of the Irish Intermediate League, he was allowed the scope to express his creativity at Goodison. Irvine loved to run defenders ragged with his breath-taking dribbling. He was capable of using both feet and the inside of his head. Despite his uncanny ability to ride tackles, the inside-right was subjected to his fair share of painful knocks. He soldiered on to become Bill Dean's first sidekick. Bill told me that he learned a lot from Irvine's desire to walk the ball into the net but never understood why he took off part way through the 1927/28 campaign. ★★ **Gordon Watson**

International appearances
during Everton career

♛ Northern Ireland: 6 caps

Pedigree

Glentoran
Everton
Nottingham Forest
Manchester United

Born: 1946
Belfast

Blue Stats

	apps	goals
League	30/2	0
FA Cup	3/1	0
Other	1/1	0
Total	34/4	0
1967/68-70/71		

Tommy Jackson only got a game when one of 'The Holy Trinity' was ruled out through injury or suspension. He impressed me as an adhesive man marker who more than made up for his meat-and-potatoes technique with honest hard work. Tommy loved to snap at the heels of more illustrious opponents. In only his second game as a full-time pro, an FA Cup semi-final clash with Leeds, he harassed Billy Bremner and Johnny Giles out of their strides. Tommy was never a weak link and provided steadfast service throughout the 1969/70 season before moving to Nottingham Forest as part of the deal which gave us Henry Newton. ★★ **Gordon Watson**

International appearances
during Everton career

♛ England: 2 caps

Pedigree

Fordingbridge Turks
Southampton
Everton
Preston North End
Southport

**Born: 1884
Fordingbridge**

Blue Stats

	apps	goals
League	125	22
FA Cup	12	3
Other	107	26
Total	244	51
1910/11-19/20		

At first, Frank Jefferis was derided as 'The King of the South'. But the scorn evaporated after he'd demonstrated his fancy footwork and his finesse at drawing opponents and threading passes down the channels. Will Cuff admitted that, even though the inside-right had been an unknown entity, he'd signed him because he played football in the Everton way. Jefferis was a quiet man who did his talking on the pitch, where he was unashamedly articulate, and developed into the hub of the 1915 title side. The burden of expectation, which had hung albatross-like around the neck of his predecessors, hardly troubled him. ★★★ **Gordon Watson**

Frank Jefferis

Blue Stats

	apps	goals
League	79/10	15
FA Cup	5	2
Other	7/2	3
Total	91/12	20
1970/71-72/73 & 82/83-83/84		

David Johnson excelled in Merseyside derbies and was the first man to net a winner for both the Blues and the Reds. As a youngster, David caught my eye with his mobility and panoramic vision. He also appeared to be blessed with the Midas touch and found the target on his Everton debuts in the League, FA Cup, League Cup and European Cup. His initial brush with fame lost its bristles and he was traded to Ipswich in exchange for Rod Belfitt. It was a pungent deal. David returned to Goodison via Anfield, where he had prospered on the domestic and European fronts, but by then he'd lost his pace as well as his cutting edge. ★ **Gordon Watson**

International appearances
during Everton career

England: 3 caps

Pedigree

Dalton Athletic
Dalton Casuals
Manchester City
Everton
Liverpool
Darwen
Notts County
Bury

**Born: 1900
Dalton in Furness**

Blue Stats

	apps	goals
League	146	56
FA Cup	13	8
Other	2	1
Total	161	65
1929/30-33/34		

'Tosh' Johnson was both a maker and a taker of goals. He could hit long balls through the eye of a needle and switch play with beautiful cross-field passes. Signed in a desperate attempt to avoid relegation in 1930, he was unable to work miracles. However, the dark clouds that had descended over Goodison quickly lifted when it became apparent that 'Tosh' and his colleagues had gelled into a team of rare quality. Flushed with confidence, Everton snapped up trophies in each of the next three seasons. Time has clouded my memory but I think that his transfer to Anfield left everyone at a loss for words. ★★★ **Gordon Watson**

Pedigree

Everton
Coventry City
Seiko
Preston North End

Born: 1956
Liverpool

Blue Stats

	apps	goals
League	79/7	1
FA Cup	5	1
Other	11/1	0
Total	95/8	2
1975/76-78/79		

David Jones was an honest lad and a natural competitor. I liked him because he tackled with extra bite and jumped with extra spring until Achilles problems hampered his progress. That said, Jones's game was not without flaws. In particular, his ball distribution let him down and comparisons have been made with David Unsworth. Some wags have unfairly claimed that giving either of them the ball was like presenting a Stradivarius to a tone-deaf gorilla. Most recently, he has bounced back from adversity to emerge as one of the best home-grown managers and a future candidate for the Goodison hot-seat. ★ **Gordon Watson**

Pedigree

Everton
Birmingham City
Fort Lauderdale Strikers

Born: 1951
Liverpool

Blue Stats

	apps	goals
League	76/6	12
FA Cup	7/2	1
Other	7	1
Total	90/8	14
1970/71-75/76		

Gary Jones was a one-off. He was a genius who upon lacing up his boots inhabited his own football galaxy where anything was possible. Jones had the sort of pizzazz that made the hairs on the back of my neck stand up. He'd the refined touch, dribbling skills and football intelligence to become another George Best. But like many before and after him, Jones failed to fulfil his potential through a mix of ill-discipline and mis-management. He never recovered from his row with Billy Bingham after being withdrawn against Leeds and was effectively expelled from the School of Science. His transfer request read more like a suicide note. ★★★★ **Gordon Watson**

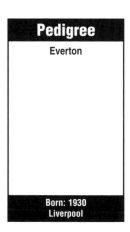
Tommy Jones was the most gallant man to have ever worn Everton's colours. Converted to a Number 5 to fill the void left by his more illustrious namesake, Tommy was a more conventional stopper. He was equipped with the strength and courage to diffuse most situations and was a model of consistency for the best part of a decade. He knew how to win, as well as lose, with dignity and is renowned for exuding decency both on and off the pitch. His impeccable sportsmanship bears up favourably to any comparison. I may be guilty of selective blindness and amnesia but I can't recall Tommy ever whacking anyone. ★★★★ **Gordon Watson**

International appearances
during Everton career

 Wales: 17 caps

Pedigree

Wrexham
Everton
Pwllhelli

**Born: 1917
Connah's Quay**

Blue Stats

	apps	goals
League	165	4
FA Cup	10	1
Other	141	29
Total	316	34
1936/37-49/50		

Forget about Bobby Moore and John Charles, TG Jones was the most polished British defender of all time. His aristocratic style and his uncommon ability to stroke the ball around when under pressure seduced football purists. TG even headed corner-kicks back to Ted Sagar. I called him 'Cryogenic Jones'. His fame spread world-wide and Everton tentatively accepted a massive bid from Roma. The transfer negotiations collapsed but his reputation lived on. I remember walking home with 'Labby' after he'd had a particularly good game only for the England centre-half to be informed by an old fan that he wasn't a patch on TG. ★★★★★ **Gordon Watson**

Pedigree

Dynamo Kiev
Shaktyor Donetsk
Manchester United
Everton
Fiorentina
Rangers
Manchester City
Southampton

Born: 1969
Kirovograd, Ukraine

Blue Stats

	apps	goals
League	52	20
FA Cup	6	1
Other	2	1
Total	60	22

1995/96-96/97

Andrei Kanchelskis was world-class. Despite his big-money move being mired by an unsavoury dispute between his former clubs, the Ukrainian wide-boy lit up Goodison with exhilarating displays of whippet-like acceleration and stunning marksmanship. Kanchelskis made the game look easy and the royal blue fraternity would hold its combined breath every time he touched the ball. Alarmingly, his Everton career faltered leading to much tittle-tattle by scandal-mongers. He gravitated to a ghost of his former self and appeared to lose interest in the club. How else can you explain his dramatic dip in form prior to his transfer to Italy?   ★★★★ Gordon Watson

International appearances
during Everton career

England: 1 cap

Pedigree

Sheffield Wednesday
Everton

Born: 1937
Sheffield

Blue Stats

	apps	goals
League	50	4
FA Cup	5	0
Other	3	0
Total	58	4

1962/63-63/64

Tony Kay was the hard-man who broke Harry Catterick's heart. The left-half was feared for his perceptive passes as much as his pulverising tackles but wasn't my kind of Blue. I thought that he was far too arrogant and was responsible for far too many flaying elbows and too many phlegm vendettas. Kay could well have taken Nobby Stiles' place in the England set-up but was banned from football for life after the match-fixing trial in 1965. He had allegedly bet on his side, Sheffield Wednesday, losing at Ipswich. It's no secret that football is far from pure. Some say that Kay was foolish, others claim that he was merely careless. ★★★ **Gordon Watson**

Theo Kelly was an ultra-efficient administrator who left his mark by designing the club's badge. Highly regarded for his business know-how and for his single-mindedness in keeping the club going during the war, Theo never saw eye-to-eye with some senior players who claimed that he'd orchestrated the departure of Bill Dean. From my extensive dealings with him, I know that Theo always put the interests of the club before those of any one individual - including himself. However, his promotion to the position of Everton's first manager was ill-conceived and he reverted to his old job as club secretary after a string of poor seasons. ★★★ **Gordon Watson**

Pedigree

Renton
Newcastle West End
Everton
Preston North End
Everton
Dundee

Born: 1865
Cardross

Blue Stats

	apps	goals
League	89	5
FA Cup	14	0
Other	0	0
Total	103	5

1888/89 & 1891/92-95/96

Bob Kelso was an uncompromising half-back cum full-back with a game based on stern and gritty tackling. He preferred to keep the ball on the floor but could also spray passes to land on the proverbial sixpence. The Scotland international's first spell at Everton was fleeting - one outing in the inaugural League campaign. After picking up championship honours with Preston, to add to those earned previously at Renton, Kelso re-joined Everton and was instrumental in the club's progress to the 1893 FA Cup final at Fallowfield. He moved back to Scotland and, nine years after gaining his first cap, received further international honours. ★★ **Gordon Watson**

Pedigree

Preston North End
Everton
Birmingham City
Stoke City
Blackburn Rovers
Everton

**Born: 1946
Ryton on Tyne**

Blue Stats

	apps	goals
League	231/3	21
FA Cup	23	3
Other	19	6
Total	273/3	30

1966/67-73/74 & 81/82

Howard Kendall was a midfield maestro whose tidy passing and brisk tackling contributed to our championship success in 1970. Astonishingly he earned no other honours and was tagged the most talented player never to have been capped. Everton fans remain puzzled by Alf Ramsey picking Peter Storey of Arsenal and John Hollins of Chelsea ahead of him. 'Kendall - the Player' was a criminally under-rated member of 'The Holy Trinity' who developed into an even better player after Alan Ball had gone. I sulked after 'Bally' left for Arsenal but must admit that I wept when Howard was sold to Birmingham. ★★★★★ **Gordon Watson**

Money can buy success but winning trophies without money brings sainthood. Howard Kendall guided us to two titles, innumerable Wembley appearances and European glory on a shoestring and put the pride back into Everton. He grasped the reins again in 1990 and 1997 but 'Kendall - the Gaffer' is most fondly remembered for his first spell in the Eighties when he shaped a mix of veterans and wannabees into the most coveted team in Europe. His squad brimmed with camaraderie and played beautiful football. Howard should be exalted for his great successes and should've been treated much better by the club in 1998. ★★★★★ Gordon Watson

Mr Howard Kendall

Pedigree

Everton
Vancouver Whitecaps
Bristol City
Altrincham

Born: 1949
Blackpool

Blue Stats

	apps	goals
League	254/14	6
FA Cup	15/1	2
Other	22/3	1
Total	291/18	9
1967/68-78/79		

Roger Kenyon was a first-class defender who was more of a Barbarian than a Corinthian. Respected for his sound distribution, impressive turn of speed and merciless tackles, he was a good captain as well as a good player whose career was undermined by injuries sustained in a car accident. Behind his back, his team-mates called him 'The Assassin' and it was rumoured that he had 'love' and 'hate' painted on his boots. In my book, Roger was the best Everton player to have been denied England honours. It was a scandal that he was named as a sub on several occasions by Don Revie only to be confined to the bench. ★★★ **Gordon Watson**

International appearances
during Everton career

England: 9 caps

Pedigree

Arsenal
Brighton & Hove Albion (loan)
Aston Villa
Everton
Arsenal

Born: 1966
Oxford

Blue Stats

	apps	goals
League	92/4	0
FA Cup	12/1	0
Other	11	0
Total	115/5	0
1989/90-92/93		

Martin Keown of Everton and England - just doesn't sound right. It took time for him to win widespread respect but Keown was capped by England during his time at Goodison. In my opinion, he seemed destined for greater international fame. The authoritative defender was bought as a ready-made replacement for Kevin Ratcliffe and was the ideal partner for Dave Watson. He was poised, intelligent and very tough. In fact, he was Colin Harvey's shrewdest acquisition. Football has always thrived on mysteries and I've never fathomed why he left so suddenly. As a rule, ambitious clubs don't sell their better players. ★★ **Gordon Watson**

Martin Keown 135

Pedigree

Manchester United
Arsenal
Manchester City
Everton
Bolton Wanderers

**Born: 1949
Manchester**

Blue Stats

	apps	goals
League	40	12
FA Cup	4	4
Other	7	4
Total	51	20
1978/79-79/80		

Having grabbed the headlines as a teenager in Manchester United's European Cup-winning side, Brian Kidd never recaptured his most exhilarating form at Everton. The athletic and skilful striker was signed by Gordon Lee to follow in the footsteps of Smallman, Pearson, McKenzie and Walsh as the elusive foil for Bob Latchford. Inexplicably, Kidd and Latchford never hit it off and Everton won only two or three of the games they played together. Ironically Kidd was more productive than his partner. To most Blues, his name is synonymous with an early bath - after he got himself sent-off in an FA Cup semi-final against West Ham. ★★ **Gordon Watson**

Andy King was one of the value-for-money buys of the twentieth century. His audacious skills thrilled the long-suffering fans in the 1970s and his up-beat nature had a similarly positive sway in the dressing room. King also had the knack of scoring stunning goals and none was more welcomed than his 20-yard volley which ended the Reds' seven-year domination of Merseyside derbies. He was sold to QPR but returned to his spiritual home two years later in the swap deal which took Peter Eastoe to West Brom. King was as irrepressible as ever and kicked-off his second spell in impressive fashion until he suffered knee damage. ★★★ **Gordon Watson**

International appearances
during Everton career

England: 26 caps

Pedigree

Everton

Born: 1940
Liverpool

Blue Stats

	apps	goals
League	451	2
FA Cup	45	0
Other	37	0
Total	533	2

1957/58-71/72

To this day, Brian Labone is extolled as 'The Last of the Corinthians'. He's the finest ambassador that any club could have and is the greatest Evertonian of the post-war era. 'Labby' possessed the essential virtues of a central kingpin - aerial dominance, strong tackling, astute positioning and constructive distribution. But I think that his good humour and sportsmanship stood him apart from his contemporaries. He was also a focal point of two championship sides and also captained our dramatic FA Cup triumph over Sheffield Wednesday in 1966. Troubled by an Achilles injury, 'Labby' retired after 15 seasons at the top. ★★★★★ **Gordon Watson**

International appearances
during Everton career

👑 England: 12 caps

Pedigree

Birmingham City
Everton
Swansea City
NAC Breda
Coventry City
Lincoln City
Newport County
Merthyr Tydfil

Born: 1951
Birmingham

Blue Stats

	apps	goals
League	235/1	106
FA Cup	17/1	10
Other	34/1	22
Total	286/3	138
1973/74-80/81		

Bob Latchford lived up to his tag of the most expensive player in the land. Signed in a deal which involved Howard Kendall and Archie Styles moving to Birmingham, the burly centre-forward was a master of burying half-chances in and around the penalty area. He was our ace striker for his eight seasons and reached the zenith of his career by plundering 30 goals in the 1977/78 campaign to claim a £10,000 prize - which he pooled with his team-mates. Latchford led the line with his own brand of hustle and bustle and, like all Blues, I deeply regret that he never had a partner who could fully capitalise on his yeoman efforts.   ★★★★★ **Gordon Watson**

Bob Latchford

Pedigree

Dumbarton Athletic
Everton
Liverpool

Born: 1867
Dumbarton

Blue Stats

	apps	goals
League	136	69
FA Cup	12	1
Other	0	0
Total	148	70
1889/90-95/96		

Alex Latta honed his skills with Dumbarton Athletic before moving south to Everton. He was our first professional import from the Scottish town which also provided Richard Boyle, John Bell, John Robertson and Jack Taylor. The outside-right had been awarded two caps and had basked in the limelight of being an exuberant showman, occasionally a show-off. Latta possessed a powerful shot and his goals helped Everton to win the League for the first time. I've been told that he was one of the outstanding personalities of early Merseyside football and, from all accounts, was something of a maverick both on and off the pitch. ★★★ **Gordon Watson**

International appearances
during Everton career

England: 8 caps

Pedigree

Burnley
Everton
Chelsea
Notts County
Brentford
Arsenal
Kettering Town

Born: 1919
Bolton

Blue Stats

	apps	goals
League	87	65
FA Cup	8	5
Other	114	152
Total	209	222
1936/37-45/46		

Tommy Lawton was a royal blue sensation - only he could have approached the standards set by Bill Dean. Tommy could knock them in from everywhere. He was outstanding in the air and was even better on the ground. Though the centre-forward always lived in the shadows of his predecessor, some fans believed that he was a more complete footballer. I'd disagree but I'm convinced that we never saw him at his peak. Tommy was just 19 when he led our title charge and then lost six years to Mr Hitler. His England record was unbelievable, netting 29 times in some 27 peace-time and war-time fixtures while on our books. ★★★★★ **Gordon Watson**

Cyril Lello was a committed club-man. I recall that Cyril was getting on a bit when he signed for us and was privileged to move into the club house in Goodison Avenue that had been previously occupied by Theo Kelly. He was a durable right-half over-reliant on biting tackles and timely interceptions. The latter was a technique that he almost got the hang of. Cyril knew his own weaknesses and never yearned to be another Cliff Britton or Joe Mercer. He was our first player to make 150 consecutive appearances. It may sound uncharitable but I suspect that he'd have struggled to have played as many games in any other era.   ★ **Gordon Watson**

International appearances
during Everton career

Sweden: 4 caps

Pedigree

Brommapojkama
Orgryte
Young Boys
Cremonese
Arsenal
Everton
Birmlngham City
Colorado Rapids
Solna

Born: 1965
Solna

Blue Stats

	apps	goals
League	51/15	5
FA Cup	7/3	1
Other	5	0
Total	63/18	6

1993/94-96/97

Anders Limpar was a rarity - a dazzling entertainer in the modern game. The left-winger had exquisite equilibrium and seemed to dribble with the ball fastened to his boots. Gwladys Street loved his flair but disapproved of his petulance. Some fans lambasted Limpar for unnecessarily conceding a penalty in the relegation epic against Wimbledon. I believe that he answered his critics in most emphatic style with his counter-attacking slaloms through the Manchester United defence at Wembley the next season. Limpar never let us down on the grand stage. Cometh the hour, cometh the television cameras, cometh the swaggering Swede. ★★ **Gordon Watson**

Pedigree

Leicester City
Everton
Barcelona
Tottenham Hotspur
Nagoya Grampus Eight

Born: 1960
Leicester

Blue Stats

	apps	goals
League	41	30
FA Cup	6	5
Other	6	3
Total	53	38
1985/86		

Gary Lineker was billed as the icing on the championship cake but is remembered as a national hero who never caught the imagination of the Goodison fraternity. Despite his searing pace and prolific marksmanship, Lineker failed to deliver the League and Cup double - both trophies being conceded to our arch-rivals. His need to receive balls in space seemed to upset the aesthetics of the championship side which had functioned so smoothly before his arrival. Perhaps Lineker was a victim of his own success. After gaining a basketful of caps and the odd golden boot, he defected to Spain. Some Blues cried: 'Adios amigo'. Others didn't.   ★★★★   **Gordon Watson**

Pedigree

Everton
Sheffield Wednesday
Grimsby Town

Born: 1951
Liverpool

Blue Stats

	apps	goals
League	364/25	48
FA Cup	29/1	6
Other	43	5
Total	436/26	59
1970/71-81/82		

Mike Lyons was born to play for Everton. Contrary to myriad misconceptions, he was a good player - no-one makes 450 appearances by good fortune - and compensated for his limitations with awesome athleticism and an unflagging appetite for hard work. Lyons threw his royal blue heart and soul into every battle and confounded his critics by emerging as a solid central defender. He was an integral part of the Goodison set-up for more than a decade and seemed to understand the passion of the fans better than any other player in the Seventies. Off the park, Lyons has always been something special - an honourable man. ★★★★ **Gordon Watson**

Pedigree

Hibernian
Everton
Swindon Town

Born: 1885
Aberdeen

Blue Stats

	apps	goals
League	245	6
FA Cup	25	1
Other	29	0
Total	299	7
1907/08-19/20		

John Maconnachie was a sophisticated defender who could excite spectators. Maconnachie played in an era when the main job of a full-back was to punt the ball as far as possible. I've been told that Goodison embraced him as a harmless eccentric who preferred to use his rich blend of skills to avert danger and construct attacks. Granted, the Everton skipper sometimes over-indulged his obsession for playing his way out of trouble and raised the blood pressure as well as the eyebrows of his colleagues. But nothing fazed him. He only seemed ruffled after coming unstuck and gifting the odd goal to opponents. ★★★ **Gordon Watson**

Mickael Madar was from another planet. Despite his heavenly first-touch and penchant for cushioned one-twos, he was no powder-puff front-man. Even though he'd been out of action for some time with a badly broken leg, Madar threw caution to the wind and helped to save our bacon by banging home half-a-dozen precious goals in 1998. On the flip-side, 'Le Bleu' became increasingly histrionic in protesting decisions and bemoaning colleagues - his tantrums becoming more frequent than his goals. The fans didn't know what to make of his alien ways but I think that he deserves a place of affection in our consciousness.

★ **Gordon Watson**

SANDON HOTEL

George Mahon orchestrated a ground-move. The organist at St Domingo Methodist church led the revolt against John Houlding to the club being headquartered at the Sandon Hotel and to the rent increases proposed for the use of the Anfield ground. Mahon drew on his business acumen as a partner in the firm of accountants, Roose, Mahon & Howarth, to organise the move to Mere Green and to raise the £3,500 required to construct Goodison. Mahon subsequently served as a director for more than a decade. I wonder what he'd have thought about the planned move to the King's Dock? I suspect he would've built it by now. ★★★★ **Gordon Watson**

International appearances
during Everton career

 England: 4 caps

Pedigree

Everton

**Born: 1881
Middlesbrough**

Blue Stats

	apps	goals
League	284	16
FA Cup	52	7
Other	0	0
Total	336	23
1902/03-14/15		

Harry Makepeace never looked like a professional athlete but he knew football inside and out. The half-back was respected for his exemplary behaviour, as well as for being composed, focussed and mentally tough, and starred in our teams which won the FA Cup in 1906 and the League title in 1915. Makepeace also earned four England caps and after World War I coached at Everton. He later concentrated on cricket and shared with Jack Sharp the rare honour of representing England at both sports. In fact, Makepeace hit the national headlines by becoming the oldest player to score a maiden Test century. ★★★★★ **Gordon Watson**

Pedigree

United Church
Everton

Born: 1858
Liverpool

Blue Stats

	apps	goals
League	0	0
FA Cup	0	0
Other	140	1
Total	140	1

1880/81-87/88

Tom Marriott helped to erect the goal posts at Stanley Park and few individuals can claim to have done more for the club. Marriott was a no-nonsense left-back who even played in goal on one occasion in 1882/83 - the season in which the club tried nine different custodians. He featured in the sides which won the Liverpool Cup in 1884 and 1886 but never appeared in the League or the FA Cup. Marriott also served as vice-captain and assistant-treasurer and upheld the virtues and values of his generation. The mists of time have obscured some of our founding fathers but I hope that he'll be included in the Hall of Fame some day. ★★ **Gordon Watson**

International appearances
during Everton career

Scotland: 2 caps

Pedigree

Ayr United
Manchester United
Everton
Liverpool
St Johnstone
Watford
New Brighton

Born: 1895
Campbeltown

Blue Stats

	apps	goals
League	97	1
FA Cup	6	0
Other	0	0
Total	103	1
1922/23-25/26		

Neil McBain was something of a chameleon. He was signed from Manchester United to take over from Tom Fleetwood as the fulcrum of the Everton defence and the deal sent shock-waves along the East Lancs Road. McBain was an elegant player who often neglected his defensive responsibilities to make daredevil surges in support of his forwards. Within a few months, his vulnerabilities had been exposed and most fans wondered what all the palaver had been about at Old Trafford. McBain later created history as the man player to appear in a League fixture, when he pulled on the keeper's jersey for New Brighton at age 52.   ★ Gordon Watson

Pedigree

Bradford City
Everton
Rangers
Bradford City

Born: 1964
Leeds

Blue Stats

	apps	goals
League	99/4	6
FA Cup	16/2	3
Other	18/1	1
Total	133/7	10
1988/89-90/91		

Stuart McCall resembled a blue-bottle. Far from being extravagantly gifted, he always showed abundant determination as we fought to keep up with our red neighbours in the late-Eighties. McCall certainly never hid and would flit from box-to-box giving everything. Unfortunately, the midfielder lacked the composure to put his foot on the ball and take stock of the game. He wasn't a prolific goal-scorer but came on as a substitute in the 1989 FA Cup final and equalised on two occasions - to no avail. I strongly believe that, in the wake of the Hillsborough disaster, the final should never have been contested that year.   ★ **Gordon Watson**

Pedigree

Airdrieonians
Everton
New Brighton

Born: 1896
Dykehead

Blue Stats

	apps	goals
League	208	0
FA Cup	16	0
Other	0	0
Total	224	0
1920/21-26/27		

John McDonald was a natural-born leader. Signed from lowly Airdrieonians, he was appointed Everton captain amid much furore. The full-back relished a scrap and everyone who came up against him knew that they'd been in one. McDonald was known for his commitment and rarely lost 50-50 balls. Coincidentally, he played at a time when Everton's socks were coloured black and blue. I've heard that he'd rouse his motley troops before battle like a medieval war-lord but in spite of his dogged efforts the club struggled during his seven seasons with us. It's fair to claim that they don't make men like him anymore - not even in Scotland.   ★★   **Gordon Watson**

Pedigree

Rangers
Everton
Accrington
Everton

Born: 1855
Ayr

Blue Stats

	apps	goals
League	0	0
FA Cup	0	0
Other	91	86
Total	91	86

1880/81-82/83 & 82/83-86/87

Jack McGill single-handedly converted Everton from a Sunday school outfit into a professional side. He introduced a more cultivated approach by emphasising team-work and patient passing. The club immediately benefited from his expertise by gaining admission to the newly-formed Lancashire FA in 1880. McGill was our first captain, first coach, first star and first unofficial professional. He was equally dextrous and played in eight different positions at a time when performances were more important than results. Some 60 years ago Will Cuff told me that Evertonians owe a huge debt to Jack McGill. We still do. ★★★★★ **Gordon Watson**

Pedigree

Nottingham Forest
Leeds United
Anderlecht
Everton
Chelsea
Blackburn Rovers
Tulsa Roughnecks
Chicago Sting
Ryoden

Born: 1950
Grimsby

Blue Stats

	apps	goals
League	48	14
FA Cup	7/1	5
Other	6	2
Total	61/1	21
1976/77-77/78		

Duncan McKenzie was magic - for a short time at least. His dazzling footwork and body-swerves seduced the fans including me. In fact, he had Gwladys Street chanting his name within minutes of his home debut against Birmingham and many thought that Billy Bingham had unearthed a latter-day Alex Young. Predictably, McKenzie suffered from playing in a dysfunctional side and his star soon waned. In no time at all, he'd been re-branded a ball-juggling novelty who drifted out of the action when things weren't going too well. I was saddened by the way in which the little magician was discarded by new manager Gordon Lee. ★★ **Gordon Watson**

Pedigree

Everton
Aston Villa
Liverpool
Manchester City

Born: 1961
Liverpool

Blue Stats

	apps	goals
League	99/1	11
FA Cup	9	0
Other	11	3
Total	119/1	14
1980/81-82/83		

Steve McMahon was a born-and-bred Evertonian who became our heart-beat while still in his teens. He was a breath of fresh air and brought a special sparkle to the midfield - something that had been absent since the days of 'The Holy Trinity'. I thought that he had it all and always gave his all. McMahon was a tenacious ball-winner as well as an expert play-maker who showed great vision and even greater determination. But he was impatient for honours and was reluctantly sold to Aston Villa. Of course, McMahon returned to haunt Goodison when he became Kenny Dalglish's first signing for Liverpool.   ★★★ **Gordon Watson**

International appearances
during Everton career

Eire: 4 caps

Pedigree

Everton
Huddersfield Town
Halifax Town
Drogheda

**Born: 1934
Dublin**

Blue Stats

	apps	goals
League	165	1
FA Cup	10	0
Other	1	0
Total	176	1
1957/58-63/64		

Mick Meagan was an affable mongrel in the kennel of pampered hounds of the Merseyside Millionaires. A product of Dublin junior football, 'Chick' survived the transformation financed by Mr Moores and remained a first-team regular for seven seasons. He certainly deserved his place in our 1963 championship-winning side which included big signings such as Alex Parker, Tony Kay, Gordon West, Roy Vernon and Alex Young. The Eire international was a dedicated pro who was at ease at full-back or half-back. He was never a world-beater but was used as the bait to entice one away from Huddersfield Town.

★★ **Gordon Watson**

International appearances
during Everton career

 England: 5 caps

Pedigree

Ellesmere Port Town
Shell Mex
Elton Green
Everton
Arsenal

**Born: 1914
Ellesmere Port**

Blue Stats

	apps	goals
League	170	1
FA Cup	14	1
Other	123	2
Total	307	4
1932/33-46/47		

Joe Mercer was the nicest man I have ever met. Joe convinced me that pain is an important part of being a Blue and throughout his life, in which he won titles with Everton and Arsenal, captained England, managed Manchester City to the top, coached the national team and was elected Footballer of the Year, he retained a near-religious devotion to the Toffees. Joe was a world-class wing-half and it was a joy to play alongside him. He made the game look deceptively easy. At the time, I considered him indispensable and never thought that we'd recover from the introspection which accompanied his departure to Highbury. ★★★★★ **Gordon Watson**

International appearances
during Everton career

 England: 4 caps

Pedigree

Old Borlasians
Great Marlow
Everton
New Brighton Tower
Southampton
New Brompton

Born: 1870
Marlow

Blue Stats

	apps	goals
League	201	85
FA Cup	23	11
Other	0	0
Total	224	96
1888/89-96/97		

Alf Milward was a gentleman amateur who was transformed into a consummate professional at Everton. Coaxed away from the playing fields of the Home Counties, he established himself as one of the most courageous forwards of his day. Will Cuff referred to him as a warrior who wore an icy camouflage of discipline - the type you'd want on your side in a battle. His partnership with Edgar Chadwick is the stuff of legend. Milward was ever-present in our first championship side but in the FA Cup he showed that losing is a difficult habit to quit, collecting runners-up medals with Everton in 1893 and 1897 and Southampton in 1902. ★★★★ **Gordon Watson**

Mr Moores was a canny chairman. The Littlewoods boss was a visionary and was committed to improving everything at the club - from the acquisition of world-class footballers to the provision of catering facilities. Mr Moores loved Everton and everyone loved him. To be honest, we were in awe of him. After all, he was the only multi-millionaire that we knew - whereas today we keep five of them on the bench. Mr Moores was fanatical about football and I can recall him at Bellefield trying to show Derek Temple how to cross the ball. As a man of ambition and integrity, he would've deemed our present woes to be totally unacceptable. ★★★★★ **Gordon Watson**

Pedigree

Liverpool
Everton
Oldham Athletic

Born: 1940
Liverpool

Blue Stats

	apps	goals
League	257/2	43
FA Cup	29	3
Other	26	4
Total	312/2	50
1962/63-71/72		

Johnny Morrissey was a hard-case from Scotland Road who made Tommy Smith and 'Chopper' Harris look tame. Only fools messed with Johnny. His ruthlessness has become a part of our folklore and I can vouch that nobody wanted to play against him in training. On the other hand, I must add that he was blessed with fabulous ball control and loved to run at - and sometimes through - defenders. Brian Labone said that Johnny needed his muscle-man physique to carry his abundance of skills and that he was arguably the best out-and-out winger in the late-Sixties. I wouldn't argue with 'Labby' nor for that matter with Johnny! ★★★★ **Gordon Watson**

Johnny Morrissey

Pedigree

Tranmere Rovers
Everton
Aston Villa
Wolverhampton Wanderers
Carlisle United
Northampton Town
Walsall

Born: 1962
Liverpool

Blue Stats

	apps	goals
League	100/6	19
FA Cup	17	2
Other	30/1	4
Total	147/7	25
1982/83-87/88		

Derek Mountfield was an endangered species - a blue-nose who wanted to play for Everton. Although only slightly-built, he developed into a fine centre-back. Mountfield's strengths were his poise on the ball and his instinct for poaching vital goals. He scored more regularly than some modern-day strikers - netting 14 times during the magnificent 1984/85 season. Few of us will forget the celebrations after his dramatic extra-time winner against Luton in the semi-final at Villa Park - his whopper of a black-eye adding to his cult-status. Sadly, debilitating cartilage injuries robbed him of a longer career in his beloved blue and white. ★★★ Gordon Watson

Pedigree

Clyde
Chelsea
Everton
Tranmere Rovers
Kilmarnock

Born: 1963
Glasgow

Blue Stats

	apps	goals
League	81/28	16
FA Cup	12/6	2
Other	18/3	3
Total	111/37	21
1988/89-91/92		

Pat Nevin was a dainty forward who flattered to deceive. Signed from Chelsea before an independent tribunal had grossly over-priced him, the Scotland winger possessed an array of tricks and, when at his best, could leave defenders floundering in his wake. In retrospect, he was an artist better suited to an earlier period. Nevin certainly wasn't equipped to plug gaps or toil in the trenches and often seemed to be a by-stander bemused at the sense of chaos around him. He'll be remembered for his semi-final winner against Norwich but, even then, his joy was overshadowed by the horrific events which unfolded at Hillsborough. ★ **Gordon Watson**

International appearances
during Everton career

England: 8 caps

Pedigree

Blackburn Rovers
Everton
Burnley

**Born: 1941
Manchester**

Blue Stats

	apps	goals
League	48/1	1
FA Cup	2	0
Other	8	0
Total	58/1	1
1969/70-71/72		

Keith Newton was a cultured right-back who was frequently played out of position at Everton. He was among the best in Europe and was widely respected for his exquisitely timed tackles and advanced reading of the game. Surprisingly, his tendency to dwell on the ball upset Harry Catterick. Newton suffered a loss of confidence after returning from Mexico, where he'd played well for England in the World Cup, and laboured to maintain a regular first-team place. He wasn't shy to complain about his lot and, with the introduction of 'Tiger' McLaughlin from Falkirk, sought fresh pastures. Let's be honest - who wouldn't have? ★★ Gordon Watson

Pedigree

Darlington
Everton
Blackpool

Born: 1897
Gateshead

Blue Stats

	apps	goals
League	188	10
FA Cup	9	0
Other	1	0
Total	198	10

1924/25-30/31

John O'Donnell was an ever-present in the 1928 championship side. He was a reluctant hero reckoned by many to be the steel reinforcing Warney Cresswell's silk. Signed to cover defensive frailties, the left-back wasn't someone who tip-toed around opponents. He liked to roar that he took no prisoners - and was true to his words. Will Cuff told me that O'Donnell could be a nasty piece of work whose abrasion bordered on violence. Apparently, he wasn't reluctant to make overly-enthusiastic challenges as well as the odd wild one. I believe that O'Donnell confirmed that footballers rarely think clearly when their fists are clenched.   ★ **Gordon Watson**

Pedigree

Everton
Stoke City
Darlington
Port Vale

**Born: 1931
Dublin**

Blue Stats

	apps	goals
League	201	0
FA Cup	12	0
Other	0	0
Total	213	0
1950/51-59/60		

Jimmy O'Neill was one of a handful of Eire internationals on our books in the 1950s and inherited Ted Sagar's green jersey. His early outings were text-book stuff. Jimmy was exceptionally safe at catching crosses as well as an acrobatic shot-stopper. Of course, he got plenty of practice playing behind a defence which wobbled from one mediocre game to another. The reality of his predicament soon caught up with him and his judgement suffered - sometimes crossing the fine line between the sublime and the ridiculous. I can still picture Jimmy patrolling his area with the countenance of somebody distressed by what he was watching.   ★★ **Gordon Watson**

International appearances
during Everton career

Scotland: 1 cap

Pedigree

Kello Rovers
Falkirk
Everton
Southport
Ballymena United

Born: 1935
Irvine

Blue Stats

	apps	goals
League	198	5
FA Cup	12	0
Other	10	0
Total	220	5
1958/59-64/65		

Alex Parker was the best right-back to have played for Everton - full-stop. He'd been a big star north of the border and it was obvious that he had a massive talent to go with his big reputation. I was impressed by his first appearance for Everton Reserves - he was a dead ringer for Frankie Vaughan. Alex also had handsome football skills and, more than anything, was acclaimed for perfecting the sliding tackle technique. He defended with grace, guile and much more. With the recruitment of Ray Wilson, we had envisioned that they would develop into a dream duo. Disappointingly, Alex and Ray played only two games together. ★★★★★ **Gordon Watson**

Pedigree

Rangers
Everton
Nottingham Forest

Born: 1891
Glasgow

Blue Stats

	apps	goals
League	84	68
FA Cup	8	3
Other	7	7
Total	99	78
1913/14-20/21		

Bobby Parker kicked off his Everton career with an avalanche of goals, scoring 10 times in his first dozen games. He teased defences with his fleetness of foot and sharpness of mind and evolved into the top scorer in the pre-World War I game. Parker's strike-rate peaked during our 1914/15 championship campaign when he hit the back of the net on 36 occasions in 35 outings. Will Cuff claimed that only injuries had prevented him from beating Bertie Freeman's record. Parker received no international honours because, at that time, the Scotland selectors ignored players who made a living in the Football League.   ★★★★★ **Gordon Watson**

Pedigree

St Lawrence CYMS
Everton
Bury

**Born: 1925
Birkenhead**

Blue Stats

	apps	goals
League	167	82
FA Cup	9	7
Other	0	0
Total	176	89
1950/51-55/56		

Some saluted John Willie Parker as the perfect partner for Dave Hickson, others ridiculed him as nothing more than a big girl's blouse. Whereas Hickson was smeared with mud and blood, his alter ego never seemed to have a hair out of place at the final whistle. Personally, I thought that he was a scavenger of opportunistic goals. Like Jimmy Greaves, John Willie was usually at the right place at the right time to toe-poke them in from close range. He rose to prominence in Division Two football and was our leading marksman in our three seasons in the lower League. Obviously, I wasn't surprised when he struggled after Hickson left. ★★ **Gordon Watson**

Pedigree

Wigan Athletic
Bournemouth
Everton

Born: 1971
Eccles

Blue Stats

	apps	goals
League	88/2	3
FA Cup	9	1
Other	8/1	0
Total	105/3	4
1994/95-97/98		

Joe Parkinson was lauded as one of Joe Royle's infamous 'Dogs of War' whose bite was far worse than his bark. The central anchor strove to do the simple things well and was respected for his unselfish commitment in every skirmish. In particular, he played a key role in destroying Spurs and Manchester United during the FA Cup run in 1995. The magnitude of his value was only fully appreciated after knee problems had forced his retirement at age 26. Badly hurt against Middlesbrough, Parkinson played out the remainder of the 1996/97 season, often in agony, as the club flirted with relegation. He was a martyr. ★★ **Gordon Watson**

Pedigree

St Johnstone
Everton
Newcastle United
Gateshead

Born: 1953
Falkirk

Blue Stats

	apps	goals
League	79/21	15
FA Cup	9	2
Other	12/2	2
Total	100/23	19
1974/75-77/78		

Jim Pearson donned his royal blue shirt with pride - but it never quite suited him. He was simply too gangly to capitalise on the loose balls bouncing off Bob Latchford. Pearson exhibited decent control and eagerly harassed defenders into making mistakes but found goals hard to come by. He eventually dropped back into the hole but by then his self-belief was as brittle as his frame. His game wasn't helped by the bile that rained from the terraces. Pearson may have missed a sitter or two but, when I think of some of our serial under-achievers of late, I sigh for men with his conviction and constitution. He never short-changed the fans.　　★ **Gordon Watson**

Pedigree

Stoke City
Everton
Aston Villa

Born: 1950
Chesterton

Blue Stats

	apps	goals
League	76	2
FA Cup	6	0
Other	11	0
Total	93	2

1976/77-78/79

Mike Pejic flaunted the most ferocious tackle in post-war football. I'd go as far as to say that the ex-England left-back was the Billy Cook of his day - a cold-blooded defender who brought extra snap to our rear-guard. His pugilist appearance was no mask. He was a hard lad who dispensed bone-crunching tackles with style. The mere sight of Pejic must have struck fear into wingers throughout the land. But the defender was no Neanderthal, he was a resourceful and talented footballer who formed a formidable alliance with right-back Colin Todd before being struck down by a spate of pelvic problems which ultimately ended his career. ★★★ **Gordon Watson**

International appearances
during Everton career

England: 3 caps

Pedigree

Blackburn Rovers
Everton
Birmingham City
Blackpool
Blackburn Rovers

Born: 1941
Blackburn

Blue Stats

	apps	goals
League	97	56
FA Cup	9	8
Other	9	6
Total	115	70
1963/64-66/67		

Fred Pickering wasn't as stylish as his 24-carat predecessor but was more effective at sticking the ball into the onion bag. The stereotypical power-house, complete with a booming right-foot shot, netted hat-tricks on his debuts for Everton and England. His impressive strike-rate earned grudging acclaim because few Blues forgave him for replacing Alex Young. Fred later suffered the whims of Harry Catterick. I recall that he'd worked hard to regain fitness after twisting a knee against Liverpool yet was axed from the Wembley side. He remained a gentleman despite his trophy cabinet containing nothing but fresh air and bitter memories. ★★★ **Gordon Watson**

Pedigree

Manchester City
Everton

Born: 1953
Manchester

Blue Stats

	apps	goals
League	52/2	6
FA Cup	5	0
Other	9	1
Total	66/2	7

1986/87-87/88

Paul Power was an ageing has-been at Maine Road who quickly blossomed into a champion at Goodison Park. Having spent more than a decade with Manchester City, the veteran all-rounder grasped the lifeline offered by Howard Kendall. His royal blue fairytale started with a Charity Shield victory at Wembley and went from strength-to-strength. Power was firm in the tackle and also liked to embark on solo runs down the left flank when deputising for Pat van den Hauwe or Kevin Sheedy. Without doubt, his maturity helped us to claim our second title in three seasons but I always suspected that his heart remained a paler shade of blue. ★★ **Gordon Watson**

International appearances
during Everton career

👑 Wales: 58 caps

Pedigree

Everton
Dundee
Cardiff City
Derby County
Chester City

**Born: 1960
Mancot**

Blue Stats

	apps	goals
League	356/3	2
FA Cup	57	0
Other	76/2	0
Total	489/5	2
1979/80-91/92		

Kevin Ratcliffe lifted our one and only European trophy. When Howard Kendall provided him with the opportunity to replace the unfortunate Billy Wright at centre-half, Ratcliffe never looked back and soon claimed the captaincy of his club and country. From what I saw of him, he was the quickest defender in the League as well as one of the toughest. Ratcliffe was well aware of his strengths and his shortcomings and if in trouble would play the simple ball to either Peter Reid or Paul Bracewell. I think that it's only right that a lifelong Blue steered Everton to winning two championships, the FA Cup and the European Cup-Winners' Cup. ★★★★★ **Gordon Watson**

 **Kevin Ratcliffe** 175

International appearances
during Everton career

England: 13 caps

Pedigree

Bolton Wanderers
Everton
Queen's Park Rangers
Manchester City
Southampton
Notts County
Bury

**Born: 1956
Huyton**

Blue Stats

	apps	goals
League	155/4	8
FA Cup	35	3
Other	39/2	2
Total	229/6	13
1982/83-88/89		

Peter Reid was Howard Kendall's most inspired signing. He was a truly magnificent mid-fielder who could win the ball, pass the ball, take men on and put his foot in. Reid - rugged by foot and mouth - became the driving force behind the most successful team in our history and captured the admiration of the Goodison fans in a manner granted to very few down the years. He was our first player to be voted Players' Player of the Year and was appointed player-coach before his exit in 1989. When I think about Reid, I believe that we made two big mistakes - we should have signed him earlier and we should never have let him go! ★★★★★ **Gordon Watson**

Kevin Richardson was one of my favourites - a terrier who, through no fault of his own, became a bit-part player on the Goodison stage. Frequently called upon to deputise for the injury prone Kevin Sheedy, he was dumped back onto the bench when Sheedy was fit. To his credit, Richardson never groaned in public and, in my mind, was far too patient for his own good. I've few doubts that he'd have been a permanent fixture in any other team. Richardson was an unerring distributor of the ball and also eclipsed others at closing down opponents. He went on to earn a second title at Arsenal and an England call-up at Aston Villa. ★★★ **Gordon Watson**

Pedigree

Swindon Town
Aston Villa
Bari
Southampton
Swindon Town
Notts County
Rangers
Everton
Huan Dao Vanguards
Tranmere Rovers

Born: 1964
Bournemouth

Blue Stats

	apps	goals
League	86/26	29
FA Cup	9/1	3
Other	16/2	8
Total	111/29	40
1992/93-96/97		

Paul Rideout was a Wembley hero in 1995. The much-travelled target-man repeated the deeds of Messrs Dean and Gray by securing the FA Cup with an impressive header. Although Rideout wasn't the quickest of forwards, some say that his speed was between his ears, he always battled manfully and was expert at holding up the ball. He shone only sporadically during his stretch at Everton, which was affected by a spate of nagging injuries. I was disappointed that Rideout failed to reach a plateau of consistency. To my surprise, he was on his way to China only 24 months after he'd tasted success in front of the twin towers.

★ **Gordon Watson**

Pedigree

Clyde
Everton
Barnsley

**Born: 1930
Glasgow**

Blue Stats		
	apps	goals
League	27	6
FA Cup	0	0
Other	0	0
Total	27	6
1959/60-60/61		

Tommy Ring was a left-winger of genuine quality. Although many had thought him to be way over-the-hill, he brimmed with vitality and Goodison rose to its feet every time he touched the ball. His hocus-pocus bamboozled markers. When he zigged, they zagged and his devastating acceleration left them chasing shadows. Tragically, the ex-Scotland star fractured a leg in a sickening collision with keeper Reg Matthews at Stamford Bridge. I know that manager Johnny Carey was absolutely gutted by the sight of both of his star wingers, Tommy and Micky Lill, hobbling around on crutches. Tommy never played for Everton again. ★★★ **Gordon Watson**

Pedigree

Edinburgh Rovers
Hibernian
Heart of Midlothian
Preston North End
Everton
Preston North End

Born: 1863
Edinburgh

Blue Stats

	apps	goals
League	19	5
FA Cup	0	0
Other	0	0
Total	19	5
1888/89		

Nick Ross was rated as among the best defenders of the nineteenth century. He captained Everton from the left-back position but played practically everywhere during our inaugural League campaign. Though he never won a sausage during his brief stint, Ross is venerated as one of our greatest signings. He buttressed our defence with his savvy tactics and impeccable timing in the tackle. Ross wasn't reluctant to mix it. His decayed teeth were almost green at the gums and he liked to hiss through them at terrified foes. Harry Cooke said that people talked in hushed tones about his death from tuberculosis at age 31. ★★★★ **Gordon Watson**

International appearances
during Everton career

 England: 2 caps

Pedigree

Everton
Manchester City
Norwich City
Bristol City

Born: 1949
Liverpool

Blue Stats

	apps	goals
League	229/3	102
FA Cup	23	9
Other	21	8
Total	273/3	119
1965/66-74/75		

I have a soft spot for Joe Royle - a truly great Evertonian who wore the famous royal blue with honour. He was absolutely superb in the air - in the Dean tradition - and his skill on the floor was remarkable for such a big man. Joe was our youngest-ever player when he debuted at Blackpool in 1966 and was still only a bairn when his 23 goals secured the 1970 championship. Back and knee injuries denied him a longer playing career. He later matured into a very good Everton manager and remains the last one to win a trophy. I was so sorry to see him leave. After all, he only wanted to buy Tore Andre Flo for next to nothing. ★★★★★ **Gordon Watson**

International appearances
during Everton career

👑 England: 4 caps

Pedigree

Thorne Colliery
Everton

**Born: 1910
Moorends**

Blue Stats

	apps	goals
League	463	0
FA Cup	32	0
Other	3	0
Total	498	0
1929/30-52/53		

Ted Sagar insisted on being called 'The Boss'. He was a cross between Neville Southall and Peter Schmeichel - a goalkeeper with lightning reflexes and exemplary handling skills who constantly yelled at his team-mates. Ted patrolled his area with supreme authority and his voice thundered above the Goodison roar. I soon learned to do things his way - and that included never knocking back-passes towards him. Having toiled in the pits at age 13, he was a tough nut who diligently served Everton for 24 years - the longest period any player had spent with one club. It was an honour to be his team-mate. ★★★★★ **Gordon Watson**

International appearances
during Everton career

 Scotland: 5 caps

Pedigree

Camelon Thistle
Bo'ness United
Rangers
Everton
Hibernian

**Born: 1936
Falkirk**

Blue Stats

	apps	goals
League	149	23
FA Cup	17	2
Other	13	2
Total	179	27
1962/63-66/67		

Alex Scott was a quick thinking and a fleet-footed winger. His pace was absolutely phenomenal and had to be seen to be believed. Known as 'Chico' to his army of adoring fans, the established Scotland international was a blur in blue. To be fair, there was nothing clever or unpredictable about his approach - he just knocked the ball past defenders and thundered by them. It was a very effective tactic for a greyhound like Alex. Interestingly, with the football world at his feet, he elected to move to Goodison in preference to White Hart Lane. Alex had no regrets because he had been crowned a champion by the end of his first season. ★★★ **Gordon Watson**

 Alex Scott

International appearances
during Everton career

Ireland: 16 caps

Pedigree

Linfield
Everton
Leeds City

Born: 1884
Belfast

Blue Stats

	apps	goals
League	251	0
FA Cup	38	0
Other	0	0
Total	289	0
1904/05-11/12		

Billy Scott set the standards for his younger brother. The Ireland goalkeeper made up for his lack of size with an abundance of agility and even more courage. He was equal to the challenges of his most intimidating adversaries. Scott was a key member of the teams which won the FA Cup in 1906 and went very close to filling the trophy cabinet with other silverware. He also enjoyed success at international level before defecting to the ill-fated Leeds City in 1912, the same year that his brother joined Liverpool. I know that Will Cuff and Bill Dean had tremendous respect for both brothers and even tried to lure Elisha away from Anfield. ★★★ **Gordon Watson**

International appearances
during Everton career

England: 3 caps

Pedigree

Halliwell Rovers
Bolton Wanderers
Halliwell Rovers
Bury
Everton
Stockport County

Born: 1878
Millom

Blue Stats

	apps	goals
League	237	84
FA Cup	32	13
Other	0	0
Total	269	97
1898/99-07/08		

Jimmy Settle was feted among the first big names of English football. The inside-left had tasted international stardom before joining Everton and was acknowledged as a master of glittering footwork and defence-splitting passes. He was only a little chap but, in the days of cow pastures and laced balls, could do things that normal players wouldn't even have tried. Jack Sharp, his team-mate in the 1906 FA Cup-winning side, enthused that Settle was most revered for his late incursions into the box and Harry Cooke, his deputy during that cup run, claimed that his low centre of gravity allowed him to lock horns with much bigger foes. ★★★★ **Gordon Watson**

International appearances
during Everton career

Scotland: 12 caps

Pedigree

Eastercraigs
Dumbarton
Everton
Oldham Athletic

**Born: 1960
Glasgow**

Blue Stats

	apps	goals
League	306/16	111
FA Cup	52/2	21
Other	67/3	27
Total	425/21	159

1979/80-90/91

Graeme Sharp ranks second on our list of goal-scorers. He scored over 150 times during his dozen seasons and many of his goals were out of this world. But there was much more to his game than his gift for the spectacular. Sharp was a team player capable of accommodating the strengths of his partners. In particular, I admired his ability to shield the ball in the tightest situations. I first bumped into him in the old 300-club on his first day and he has never ceased to impress me. Of course, Sharp will always be celebrated for his goal at Anfield in 1984. It was a missile with *'Greetings from Gwladys Street'* engraved on it. ★★★★★ **Gordon Watson**

International appearances
during Everton career

England: 2 caps

Pedigree

Hereford Thistle
Aston Villa
Everton

**Born: 1878
Hereford**

Blue Stats

	apps	goals
League	300	68
FA Cup	42	12
Other	0	0
Total	342	80
1899/1900-09/10		

Jack Sharp was a flyer blessed with brilliant ball control. The powerfully-built winger also showed guts, intelligence and classic dexterity in everything that he did. He was the man-of-the-match in the 1906 FA Cup final and was also awarded two England caps. But his true love was cricket. Sharp was a mainstay in the Lancashire team for two decades and earned three England caps. He was elected to the Everton board in 1922 and no-one was signed without him vetting them. I knew him best as a club director who loved to wallow in our rich traditions as well as a shrewd businessman who ran a sports outfitting business in the city centre. ★★★★★ **Gordon Watson**

International appearances
during Everton career

 Eire: 41 caps

Pedigree

Hereford United
Liverpool
Everton
Newcastle United
Blackpool

Born: 1959
Builth Wells

Blue Stats

	apps	goals
League	263/12	66
FA Cup	38	15
Other	57/1	15
Total	358/13	96
1982/83-91/92		

Kevin Sheedy had a magic wand for a left peg. The repentant ex-Red used it to score some explosive goals as well as create thousands of opportunities for his team-mates. I'd say that 'Sheeds' was the best dead-ball specialist that I've ever seen and was capable of dispatching free kicks and corners with surgical precision. I recollect him re-taking a free-kick against Ipswich after having found the top corner. He hit the back of the net again the second time around - in the opposite corner. Evertonians expected nothing less from him but I reacted by punching the air so many times that it almost turned black and blue. ★★★★ **Gordon Watson**

International appearances
during Everton career

♛ Wales: 4 caps

Pedigree

Wrexham
Everton

Born: 1953
Connah's Quay

Blue Stats

	apps	goals
League	19/2	6
FA Cup	0	0
Other	5/1	1
Total	24/3	7
1974/75-76/77		

David Smallman was a striker of rare potential. There was something very special about the Wales ace - he seemed to make himself that extra nano-second of time to deliver his killer finish. The word on the Bellefield grapevine was that he'd dovetailed perfectly with Bob Latchford until his lot was sabotaged by premature wear and tear. If it wasn't a damaged shoulder, it was a fragile hamstring or a bad knee. He even fractured a leg. Some labelled it 'The Hoodoo of the Seventies' and at one time we had John Connolly, Gary Jones and Smallman out of action with career-threatening injuries. I still mourn the loss of his rare talent. ★★ **Gordon Watson**

David Smallman 189

Blue Stats

	apps	goals
League	142/6	3
FA Cup	26	2
Other	19/4	2
Total	187/10	7
1986/87-94/95		

Ian Snodin chose Everton over Liverpool. He'd been expected to move from Elland Road to Anfield but at the last minute opted for Goodison and was rewarded with a League medal - but very little else. An elegant footballer with a very competitive edge, Snodin was also a fine athlete. But for some reason he tended to struggle in the midfield battlefield - only to discover his niche at right-back, where he rarely wasted a ball. I would've predicted that he was destined for full international honours until his progress was blighted by persistent hamstring problems. As a consequence, Snodin had to sit out the best part of two seasons.   ★ **Gordon Watson**

International appearances
during Everton career

Wales: 92 caps

Pedigree

Llandudno Swifts
Conwy United
Bangor City
Winsford United
Bury
Everton
Port Vale
Southend United
Stoke City
Torquay United
Bradford City

Born: 1958
Llandudno

Blue Stats

	apps	goals
League	578	0
FA Cup	70	0
Other	103	0
Total	751	0
1981/82-97/98		

Neville Southall was the best in the world and our first player to be voted Footballer of the Year. 'Big Nev' was renowned for making point-blank blocks and, like all truly great keepers, for commanding his area. Often a lighthouse against the storm, guiding his defenders to safety, he demanded perfection from those in front of him. Southall was our unopposed Number 1 for more than 14 years and played more games for his club and country than any other blueblood. 'Big Nev' had such an aura of invincibility that it was possible to forget that he was human. That said, I've never understood his half-time protest against Leeds. ★★★★★ **Gordon Watson**

Pedigree

Blackburn Olympic
Blackburn Rovers
Everton

Born: 1866
Blackburn

Blue Stats

	apps	goals
League	31	36
FA Cup	1	0
Other	0	0
Total	32	36

1893/94-94/95

Prior to joining Everton, Jack Southworth had been the sparkling star of the early professional era. The England centre-forward had picked up two FA Cup winners' medals with Blackburn Rovers and had earned a nation-wide reputation as a prolific scorer. He hit his peak over the 1893 Christmas holidays with a staggering haul of 10 goals in seven days. Everton dominated the title race for most of the following season until Southworth was seriously injured against Sunderland. He never played football again. I've learned that after retiring, Southworth became a violinist with the Hallé and Liverpool Philharmonic orchestras. ★★★★ **Gordon Watson**

Pedigree

Leeds United
Everton
Newcastle United

**Born: 1969
Mancot**

Blue Stats

	apps	goals
League	58	15
FA Cup	2	1
Other	5	1
Total	65	17
1996/97-97/98		

Gary Speed deserves to be given the benefit of the doubt by Gwladys Street. The life-long Blue was a powerful midfielder equipped with a terrific left-foot shot and tremendous aerial prowess. However as club captain, he seemed to become brassed off with the mediocrity which had engulfed the club, not to mention the murkier goings-on behind the scenes, and was banished to Newcastle. But Speed was no badge-kissing Judas Escariot. I'm convinced that he aways tried to do his best for Everton. Inevitably, the rumour mill went into overdrive but true Blues need to pinch themselves and remember that he is one of us.   ★★ **Gordon Watson**

Pedigree

Dunfermline Athletic
Everton
Burnley
New Brighton

Born: 1907
Coatbridge

Blue Stats

	apps	goals
League	199	57
FA Cup	16	8
Other	2	0
Total	217	65
1928/29-34/35		

Jimmy Stein played a key role in our all-conquering teams in the early-1930s. He was respected for his sheer pace and his ability to ride tackles. When not providing generous service to Bill Dean, Jimmy loved to cut inside to deliver telling strikes. His powerful shooting resulted in a rich harvest of goals including the opener in the 1933 FA Cup final at Wembley. I remember Jimmy as an unassuming pro who towards the end of his stay was required to contest his first-team spot with up-and-coming starlets such as Jackie Coulter and Torry Gillick. He never complained and preferred to share with them the richness of his experiences. ★★★ **Gordon Watson**

Pedigree

Burnley
Everton
Rangers
Marseille
Rangers

**Born: 1963
Berwick upon Tweed**

Blue Stats

	apps	goals
League	210/4	48
FA Cup	33	4
Other	52	8
Total	295/4	60
1983/84-88/89		

Trevor Steven was more than just tricky - he was one of the most intelligent footballers that we've ever had on our books. I liked his direct approach and the fact that he didn't waste time beating defenders twice. Steven was a vital supply line for Sharp, Gray, Lineker and friends, and could also find the target himself. In fact, he finished top-scorer at the end of the 1986/87 title campaign. And who will forget the deafening roar that followed his goal against Bayern Munich? It was a gloomy day when he joined Rangers. I felt that the £1.5 million fee was insulting given that he later moved to France for three times that paltry sum. ★★★★ **Gordon Watson**

Trevor Steven

Pedigree

Bolton Wanderers
Everton
Oldham Athletic
Tranmere Rovers

Born: 1933
Dudley

Blue Stats

	apps	goals
League	120	20
FA Cup	10	1
Other	15	2
Total	145	23
1961/62-65/66		

Dennis Stevens was a midfield general who was at least a decade ahead of his time. A cousin of Old Trafford legend Duncan Edwards, Dennis had helped Bolton to win the FA Cup in 1958. His arrival at Goodison was controversial in that it hastened the departure of Bobby Collins to Leeds. Dennis proved to be a top-class ball-winner adept at supplying quality passes to his more illustrious team-mates and his unselfish running ensured that we captured the League title in 1963. I recall that he was an ever-present that season and that he preferred to move on to Oldham rather than obstruct the progress of young Colin Harvey. ★★★ **Gordon Watson**

International appearances
during Everton career

 England: 26 caps

Pedigree

Everton
Rangers
Tranmere Rovers

**Born: 1963
Barrow in Furness**

Blue Stats

	apps	goals
League	207/1	8
FA Cup	38	2
Other	47	2
Total	292/1	12
1981/82-87/88		

Gary Stevens was a top drawer defender but I've always found it hard to accept that he won the same number of caps as Brian Labone. Of course, he benefited from playing in a very good Everton side but even so had to be a very good player to keep his place in that team. Stevens rose through the ranks to claim the right-back berth and played a vital part in our success in the Eighties. He personified the modern full-back and used his rip-roaring pace to augment his forwards. With hindsight, I think that he was unduly criticised for his one sloppy pass in the 1986 FA Cup final which tilted the pendulum towards Liverpool. ★★★ **Gordon Watson**

International appearances
during Everton career

 Northern Ireland
& Eire: 20 caps

Pedigree

Dublin Dolphins
Rangers
Everton

**Born: 1912
Dublin**

Blue Stats

	apps	goals
League	255	82
FA Cup	16	8
Other	208	91
Total	479	181
1933/34-48/49		

Pound for pound, Alex Stevenson was one of the best ball-players of his era. The inside-forward packed a rich assortment of talents into his compact frame and was tough enough to withstand the most chilling tackles. In particular, Alex displayed immaculate ball control and was the brains behind our domination of Division One before the war. His speedy criss-crossing with Jackie Coulter and Wally Boyes tore defences to shreds. Alex loved everything about Everton and I fondly remember meeting him at his petrol station in Great Howard Street after he'd hung up his boots. We chatted for hours replaying our best games kick-by-kick. ★★★★★ **Gordon Watson**

Pedigree

Chelsea
Everton
Sheffield United
Charlton Athletic

Born: 1970
London

Blue Stats

	apps	goals
League	116/20	22
FA Cup	10/3	5
Other	11/1	4
Total	137/24	31
1993/94-97/98		

Graham Stuart was the diamond geezer for the big occasion. He was an adaptable player and alternated between ball-winner, match-winner and substitute - but was seldom a clinical finisher. Stuart confirmed my assessment by miscuing on two memorable afternoons. At Wembley in May 1995, he shanked his shot against the Manchester United bar with the goal beckoning. Fortunately Paul Rideout nodded home the rebound. Twelve months earlier at Goodison, with Everton needing a miracle to avoid the drop, Stuart scuffed the ball past the Wimbledon keeper. Thank you - Graham Stuart. God bless you - Hans Segers.

★ **Gordon Watson**

Pedigree

Everton
Crewe Alexandra

Born: 1929
Liverpool

Blue Stats

	apps	goals
League	133	0
FA Cup	9	0
Other	0	0
Total	142	0
1952/53-59/60		

Jimmy Tansey upheld the values of his generation by rolling up his sleeves and getting stuck in. He was the embodiment of the club in the Fifties by making the most of his austere assets and never shunning hard-work. Jimmy was a good-humoured sportsman who stalked wingers with his honest tackling. The left-back was rarely found wanting and even managed to contain Stan Matthews and Tom Finney on occasions. More than anything, he strove to ensure that we never again sank into the cold waters of Division Two. In doing so, Jimmy accepted the bouquets and brickbats from the crowd with cultivated self-mocking. ★ **Gordon Watson**

Pedigree

Newtown Thistle
Dumbarton Athletic
Paisley St Mirren
Everton
South Liverpool

Born: 1872
Dumbarton

Blue Stats

	apps	goals
League	400	66
FA Cup	56	14
Other	0	0
Total	456	80
1896/97-09/10		

Jack Taylor was one of the most respected club captains of all time. Nobody dared let him down. Jack Sharp claimed that Taylor was a natural leader who extracted the very best from his men. He was no mean player either and his football brain coupled with his unbridled enthusiasm equipped him to play anywhere. History books show that Taylor featured in the 1897 FA Cup final at outside-right and the 1906 and 1907 finals at centre-half. His playing days were curtailed after he sustained serious damage to his larynx in a semi-final replay some years later. It was a tragedy of operatic proportions for both the player and his club. ★★★★★ **Gordon Watson**

International appearances
during Everton career

♛ England: 1 cap

Pedigree

Everton
Preston North End
Wigan Athletic

Born: 1938
Liverpool

Blue Stats

	apps	goals
League	231/1	72
FA Cup	21	8
Other	24	4
Total	276/1	84

1956/57-67/68

Derek Temple earned an eternal place in Everton folklore. I first caught a glimpse of him as a schoolboy phenomenon who couldn't stop scoring. Derek matured into an exciting footballer capable of slotting into all the forward positions. He was very mobile and possessed a terrific right foot. Of course, the highlight of his career came towards the end of the 1966 FA Cup final after we'd fought back from a 2-0 deficit. Derek latched onto a defensive error and carried the ball half the length of the Wembley pitch before blasting an unstoppable shot past Ron Springett, the Sheffield Wednesday keeper. It was no fluke. ★★★ **Gordon Watson**

Blue Stats

	apps	goals
League	71	4
FA Cup	2	0
Other	11	2
Total	84	6
1977/78-78/79		

Dave Thomas enhanced the club's reputation for fielding the best wide-men that money could buy. I remember Goodison buzzing in anticipation of his arrival. He was an ace at sprinting to the by-line before releasing perfectly-weighted crosses towards Bob Latchford or cutting inside to attack the goal. The sight of Thomas in full flow with no shin-pads, socks rolled down and defenders snapping at his heels was exhilarating. Strangely, the Thomas-Latchford union won many friends but no silverware. After he'd departed to Wolves, I was left to wonder how we'd allowed such a remarkable talent to slip through our grasp. ★★★ **Gordon Watson**

International appearances
during Everton career

Scotland: 1 cap

Pedigree

Thornton Rangers
Dundee
Everton

Born: 1906
Thornton

Blue Stats

	apps	goals
League	272	5
FA Cup	22	0
Other	10	0
Total	304	5
1929/30-41/42		

'Jock' Thomson played for the jersey. Signed from Dundee in 1930, he was thrown in at the deep end of a relegation dog-fight and, in spite of his brave efforts, Everton were demoted for the first time. Predictably, 'Jock' turned things around and in no time was celebrating promotion to the top flight, a League championship and a Wembley triumph. He was a team-player and took it upon himself to look after his mates. On my debut at Brentford, 'Jock' made the hardest tackle I'd ever seen or heard. The earth shook and I still grimace thinking about it. He earned one cap but was never picked again after putting through his own goal. ★★★★★ **Gordon Watson**

204　'Jock' Thomson

Blue Stats

	apps	goals
League	32	1
FA Cup	1	0
Other	2	0
Total	35	1
1978/79-79/80		

Even though Colin Todd was the most distinguished British sweeper to have played the game, Gordon Lee persevered with the Lyons-Wright axis and deployed him at right-back. Perhaps, Todd was an embarrassment of riches. He had poise and assurance on the ball in addition to courage and timing in the tackle. Todd also displayed a huge football IQ, gained as a League championship-winner with Derby County and as a foundation stone of the England set-up. Gordon Lee should have built a side around him but, after a difference of opinion, packed him off to Birmingham. True to form, the fans were left in the dark. ★★★ **Gordon Watson**

Pedigree

Plymouth Argyle
Everton
Portsmouth
Torquay United

Born: 1944
Gunnislake

Blue Stats

	apps	goals
League	11	3
FA Cup	2	2
Other	1	0
Total	14	5

1965/66-67/68

Mike Trebilcock was one of the most unlikely heroes in the illustrious history of the FA Cup final. The little sharp-shooter possessed a modest degree of craftsmanship and even less experience but seized his 15 or so minutes in the spotlight at Wembley in 1966. His brace of goals against Sheffield Wednesday, both firmly-drilled from the edge of the penalty area, paved the way for an epic fight-back straight out of the pages of *Roy of the Rovers*. Two years after his fairy-tale performance, Mike was transferred to Portsmouth and later emigrated down-under to Australia. He confirmed that glory is fleeting but obscurity is forever.   ★ **Gordon Watson**

International appearances
during Everton career

 Scotland: 1 cap

Pedigree

Forfar Athletic
Dundee
Everton
Dundee

Born: 1895
Forfar

Blue Stats

	apps	goals
League	249	32
FA Cup	10	3
Other	1	0
Total	260	35
1922/23-29/30		

Alec Troup was Bill Dean's favourite outside-left - the only one who could consistently deliver the ball with the lace positioned away from his forehead. Troup overcame the handicap of a weak collarbone, which had to be strapped before every game, to enthral the Goodison faithful with his dazzling ball control and extra-ordinary crossing skills. The legendary centre-forward recognised the immense debt that he owed the little winger and often referred to his crosses as manna from heaven. Most appropriately, it was from one of Troup's beautifully-flighted corners that Bill headed his record-breaking sixtieth goal. ★★★ **Gordon Watson**

Pedigree

Birmingham City
Everton
Tottenham Hotspur
Millwall

Born: 1960
Dendermonde, Belgium

Blue Stats

	apps	goals
League	134/1	2
FA Cup	30	1
Other	35/1	0
Total	199/2	3
1984/85-88/89		

Pat van den Hauwe was a bully with a questionable passport. Born in Belgium and raised in London, he somehow qualified to play for Wales. The left-back was a volatile character who seemed to enjoy his reputation as one of the meanest defenders in Europe. Dubbed 'Psycho Pat' by the fans, he was a fine athlete who was good enough in the air to double as a central defender. To his credit, van den Hauwe played his part in the glory years. But he wasn't my cup of tea. Too many of his tackles were tardy. I'd go as far as to say that he lacked the football manners traditionally associated with the blue and white of Everton. ★★ **Gordon Watson**

International appearances
during Everton career

Wales: 13 caps

Pedigree

Blackburn Rovers
Everton
Stoke City
Halifax Town

Born: 1937
Ffynnongroew

Blue Stats

	apps	goals
League	176	101
FA Cup	12	7
Other	14	3
Total	202	111
1959/60-64/65		

'Taffy' Vernon was the best finisher that I had the good fortune to coach. He was very quick in short spurts and, despite his pipe-cleaner build, packed a right-foot shot of pure venom. 'Taffy' always struck with minimum back-lift and made very clean contact at the belly of the ball. Not surprisingly, he developed into an outstanding penalty-taker and converted all but one of his spot-kicks. 'Taffy' had little difficulty in bagging his quota of 20 goals per season and finished top scorer in each of his four seasons. I take great pride in knowing that I taught him how to tame the ball. I only wish I could've tamed his temper too. ★★★★★ **Gordon Watson**

Pedigree

Everton

Born: 1902
Liverpool

Blue Stats

	apps	goals
League	117	2
FA Cup	9	1
Other	1	0
Total	127	3

1924/25-29/30

Albert Virr liked to stamp his authority on proceedings. The strapping half-back had a presence, almost an arrogance, often detected in top players. Virr was a dominant figure in the 1927/28 side and provided the groundwork for the majestic wing-play of Alec Troup and Ted Critchley. He preferred to play simple but effective short passes. Lamentably, a serious knee injury forced his retirement while in his prime. Tom McIntosh noted that Virr's career had mixed the perfume of success with the faint odour of under-achievement yet believed that the delay in finding a suitable replacement contributed to our disastrous 1929/30 season. ★★★ **Gordon Watson**

Pedigree

Everton
Rochdale

Born: 1924
Southport

Blue Stats

	apps	goals
League	207	68
FA Cup	21	8
Other	66	36
Total	294	112
1943/44-55/56		

Eddie Wainwright was a scrawny forward with a healthy appetite for goals. Our paths crossed during the war and I quickly realised that his puny build was misleading. Eddie brimmed with self-belief and his beautiful balance allowed him to bounce off defenders. He blossomed into a prolific goal-scorer and represented the Football League in 1950. Other honours seemed to be on the horizon until he suffered a broken leg later that year. It was so sad to witness the unravelling of real promise and expectation. Eddie deserved an extra dollop or two of luck but at least was spared most of our time in Division Two.   ★ **Gordon Watson**

International appearances
during Everton career

 Poland: 9 caps

Pedigree

Gornik Zabrze
Everton
PHSC Foran

Born: 1963
Wielun, Poland

Blue Stats

	apps	goals
League	51/21	6
FA Cup	1/3	0
Other	8/2	2
Total	60/26	8
1990/91-93/94		

Robert Warzycha was a quality import. Known in an inoffensive sort of way as 'Bob the Pole', he was an orthodox winger who oozed style during his honeymoon under Howard Kendall. Warzycha had the power, pace and magnetic ball skills to breeze past defenders and could beat man after man with ease. He was among the most talented wide-men to have played for us in the post-war years. Warzycha also packed a wicked shot and even scored at Wembley - albeit in our Zenith Data Systems Cup debacle. Much was expected of him but for some reason he lost his hunger and his extraordinary talent was allowed to drift away.   ★★ **Gordon Watson**

International appearances
during Everton career

 England: 6 caps

Pedigree

Liverpool
Norwich City
Everton

Born: 1961
Liverpool

Blue Stats

	apps	goals
League	419/4	23
FA Cup	48	5
Other	56/1	10
Total	523/5	38
1986/87-97/98		

Dave Watson was a tremendous centre-half in the good times and the bad. 'Waggie' was such a dedicated servant that most Evertonians have expunged from their memories the fact that he'd once made the short journey across Stanley Park albeit via Carrow Road. He had few equals in the air and did the simple things effectively on the deck. Consequently, most of his outings were near-flawless. 'Waggie' was a loyal club-man who embraced every challenge that came his way at Goodison - as captain, caretaker-manager and player-coach. Who can forget his immense pleasure after receiving the FA Cup from Prince Charles? ★★★★★ Gordon Watson

International appearances
during Everton career

 England: 3 caps

Pedigree

Blackpool
Everton
Tranmere Rovers

Born: 1943
Barnsley

Blue Stats

	apps	goals
League	335	0
FA Cup	40	0
Other	27	0
Total	402	0
1961/62-72/73		

Gordon West demonstrated that a goalkeeper can be just as much a match-winner as a forward. He was the most expensive keeper in the world at age 18 and displayed breath-taking reflexes and unruffled assurance with crosses throughout his career. Gordon established a good-natured rapport with Merseyside fans of all persuasions and, during his dozen seasons with Everton, won two League titles, the FA Cup and a few handbags from his friends on the Kop. His consistency brought him to the attention of Sir Alf Ramsey but, for the life of me, I don't know why the proud patriot declined to go to the 1970 World Cup.   ★★★★ **Gordon Watson**

International appearances
during Everton career

England: 1 cap

Pedigree

Southport
Everton
Northampton Town
New Brighton

**Born: 1908
Manchester**

Blue Stats

	apps	goals
League	193	66
FA Cup	9	0
Other	2	0
Total	204	66
1927/28-36/37		

Tommy White was a big man who could play at the back as well as up front - and scored goals from both positions. His massive physique was key to his style of play. As a pivot, he was a tower of strength feared for his fierce tackling and few forwards got the better of him. At the other end of the pitch, Tommy developed into a formidable deputy for Bill Dean and was a real menace in the air. Irrespective of where he played, he gave 100% commitment. Tommy was selected for England duty in 1933. He was overwhelmed by the honour and kept his treasured cap in pristine condition in the original box wrapped in the original tissue paper. ★★★ **Gordon Watson**

Pedigree

Manchester United
Everton

Born: 1965
Belfast

Blue Stats

	apps	goals
League	27/2	9
FA Cup	6	3
Other	2	1
Total	35/2	13
1989/90-90/91		

Even though Norman Whiteside had denied us the treble, Evertonians were quick to forgive him for his extra-time winner at Wembley. In fact, his arrival from Manchester United sent waves of trepidation throughout Merseyside. Originally a winger, Whiteside's loss of pace precipitated his conversion into a midfield bodyguard who boasted a unique blend of delicate skills and brutal aggression. Tragically, he was troubled by knee injuries throughout his stay at Goodison and had to retire at age 26. Some will remember him for commitment, others for his off-the-field escapades, whereas I still curse his act of larceny in May 1985. ★★ **Gordon Watson**

Pedigree

Everton
Crystal Palace
Leyton Orient
Bournemouth

Born: 1950
Liverpool

Blue Stats

	apps	goals
League	72/2	21
FA Cup	6	2
Other	8/1	3
Total	86/3	26
1967/68-72/73		

Alan Whittle could've been a superstar. Heralded as Harry Catterick's greatest discovery of all time, Alan was such an outstanding prospect that the manager shunned buying Bolton's Francis Lee and Leicester's Allan Clarke. The teenager repaid his manager's faith by wrapping up the 1970 League title with 11 goals in a 15-game purple patch. Alan was a brash so-and-so who irritated defenders like an angry wasp. His sting became less deadly after defences grew familiar with his wares and his shine faded in anti-climax. Obviously too much was expected of him. Alan was sold to Crystal Palace among much unfounded rumour.   ★★★ **Gordon Watson**

International appearances
during Everton career

Wales: 6 caps

Pedigree

Swansea Town
Everton
Newport County

**Born: 1900
Penhriwceiber**

Blue Stats

	apps	goals
League	131	0
FA Cup	8	0
Other	1	0
Total	140	0
1929/30-35/36		

Ben Williams led Everton back into the big League and also featured prominently in the 1932 championship side. The full-back bubbled with vigour and confidence until he was struck down by a knee injury during the following campaign. Will Cuff swiftly replaced him with Billy Cook from Celtic and, rather than being left out in the cold, Ben decided to move back to Wales. Ironically, he re-surfaced to undermine our ambitions in 1937. While captaining his country against Northern Ireland, Ben broke Jackie Coulter's leg. It was a freak accident. I recall that they had been close friends and had previously shared digs together.   ★★ **Gordon Watson**

International appearances
during Everton career

 England: 33 caps

Pedigree

Huddersfield Town
Everton
Oldham Athletic
Bradford City

**Born: 1934
Shirebrook**

Blue Stats

	apps	goals
League	114/2	0
FA Cup	26	0
Other	11/1	0
Total	151/3	0
1964/65-68/69		

Ray Wilson was our very own World Cup hero. In my judgement, he was the best left-back to have played for England and was comparable in ability to the great Nilton Santos of Brazil. Ray was perfection in a Number 3 shirt and never failed to impress me with his intelligent anticipation of developing situations. His other impeccable credentials included blistering pace and ice-cool confidence under pressure. Brian Labone confessed to me that if he was in trouble he'd get the ball to Ray who was guaranteed to get him out of the jam. Inevitably Ray will be remembered for his England heroics in 1966 - he should've been knighted. ★★★★★ **Gordon Watson**

 Ramon Wilson 219

Pedigree

Horwich
Everton
Blackburn Rovers
Croydon Common
Norwich City

Born: 1879
Little Lever

Blue Stats

	apps	goals
League	160	8
FA Cup	10	0
Other	0	0
Total	170	8

1897/98-1903/04

Sam Wolstenholme was one of the finest half-backs at the turn-of-the-century. Unlike many of his peers, he wasn't the type to throw his weight around. Wolstenholme was a cultured player who passed the ball with smoothness and preferred to rely on his intuition to break up attacks rather than turf-gouging tackles. Amazingly, he was transferred to Blackburn Rovers shortly after making his international debut. Wolstenholme enjoyed a spell playing in the Southern League before moving to the continent. I've been told that he was still coaching in Germany when World War I was declared and was interned as a prisoner of war. ★★ Gordon Watson

International appearances
during Everton career

Scotland: 3 caps

Pedigree

East Stirling
Blackpool
Everton
Arsenal
Crystal Palace
Cardiff City
Blackpool
Hereford United
Merthyr Tydfil
Inter-Cardiff

Born: 1952
Douglas

Blue Stats

	apps	goals
League	103	0
FA Cup	4	0
Other	19	0
Total	126	0

1977/78-79/80

George Wood was a giant signed from Blackpool but was no Gordon West. Incredibly agile for such a big goalkeeper, Wood played well enough at Everton to launch his international career but never showed the dominance necessary to secure long-term tenure of the Number 1 jersey. He was an excellent shot-stopper but sometimes fumbled even the most harmless of crosses. As a consequence, he was forced to fight for his place with Martin Hodge. Neither of them won and Jim McDonagh was recruited from Bolton Wanderers. Wood subsequently moved on to Arsenal where he somehow kept Pat Jennings on the side-lines. ★ **Gordon Watson**

Pedigree

Everton
Birmingham City
Chester City
Carlisle United
Morecambe

Born: 1958
Liverpool

Blue Stats

	apps	goals
League	164/2	10
FA Cup	13	0
Other	19	0
Total	196/2	10

1977/78-82/83

What can I say about Billy Wright? He should've joined Weight-Watchers instead of Birmingham City on a free transfer. His excess poundage denied him a glittering career and also deprived Everton of the services of a potential England centre-half. Although Wright lacked the pace of his uncle Tommy, he was an equally polished defender who earned Under-21 honours after only a handful of League games. In fact, he looked earmarked for greatness. But the life-long Blue loved his nosh and was axed by Howard Kendall for being eight pounds heavier than decreed. He never played for Everton again - it was such a shocking waste.   ★ **Gordon Watson**

International appearances
during Everton career

 England: 11 caps

Pedigree
Everton
Born: 1944
Liverpool

Blue Stats

	apps	goals
League	307/1	4
FA Cup	35	0
Other	30	0
Total	372/1	4
1964/65-72/73		

Tommy Wright was a top-class defender who was more than a match for any forward in the land. In particular, I recall that he regularly subdued George Best. Tommy monopolised the right-back position for the best part of a decade and liked to mix his defensive duties with intelligent overlapping runs. Absolutely no-one could beat him for pace and his performances were rewarded by Alf Ramsey. Tommy showed no nerves at international level and blossomed in the 1970 World Cup, playing an absolute blinder against Brazil. Although injury forced him out of football at age 28, Tommy attends every Everton home game. ★★★★★ **Gordon Watson**

Tommy Wright

International appearances
during Everton career

Scotland: 2 caps

Pedigree

Heart of Midlothian
Everton
Glentoran
Stockport County

**Born: 1937
Loanhead**

Blue Stats

	apps	goals
League	227/1	77
FA Cup	25/2	4
Other	20	8
Total	272/3	89
1960/61-67/68		

Alex Young was exalted as 'The Golden Vision'. Although plagued by blistered feet and hearing problems, the godlike Number 9 bamboozled opponents with his divine footwork. His game was a collage of graceful first-touches, deft back-heels, delicate feints and majestic body swerves. The fans were besotted. It was hero-worship on a par with Beatlemania. Alex was undoubtedly the most idolised footballer of the twentieth century and still exerts a mythical appeal among those of the royal blue persuasion. His reception at the Hall of Fame Gala confirmed that he is adored today as much as during the golden Sixties. ★★★★★ **Gordon Watson**

International appearances
during Everton career

 Scotland: 2 caps

Pedigree

St Mirren
Falkirk
Everton
Tottenham Hotspur
Manchester City
South Liverpool

Born: 1880
Slamannan

Blue Stats

	apps	goals
League	275	110
FA Cup	39	15
Other	0	0
Total	314	125
1901/02-10/11		

'Sandy' Young was a potent hit-man whose goal in the 1906 FA Cup final sent Merseyside crazy. The stylish centre-forward was famed for his clever footwork, like his namesake from a later era, and his sublime dribbling skills bewildered more physically imposing defenders. However, he suffered from the occasional tendency to take on one defender too many. Young was troubled by periods of ill-health but, when fully fit was one of the best centre-forwards of all time. He emigrated to Australia in 1914 and the following year was charged with the murder of his brother. Some books claim that Young was found guilty of manslaughter. ★★★★ **Gordon Watson**

Hey sarge, how come we have to deal with Duncan Ferguson's contract?

Home Of The Blues

Pedigree

Halmstad
IFK Gothenburg
Sheffield Wednesday
Everton

Born: 1971
Halmstad, Sweden

Evertonians expect their heroes to have faces drenched in blood, legs caked in mud and shirts soaked in sweat. Granted Niclas Alexandersson never met these traditional expectations but was effective - on paper. End-of-season post-mortems show that the entrepreneurial Swede made more tackles, got in more crosses and took nearly as many shots as any other Everton player - though not many actually registered. For Evertonians, quality must always come ahead of quantity. It's Sod's Law, of course, that he shone for Sweden in the 2002 World Cup.

Wally Fielding

International appearances
during Everton career

 England: 1 cap

Pedigree		
Everton		
Rangers		
Born: 1979		
Liverpool		

Blue Stats		
	apps	goals
League	102/19	8
FA Cup	7/1	0
Other	7/3	0
Total	116/23	8
1996/97-2000/01		

Michael Ball could've starred in our 1998 FA Youth Cup-winning side but had already been pushed into the big time. His ability on the ball reminded me of Colin Todd. Yet the classy defender, who has the genuine blue stuff pumping through his body, was often at odds with the club management and never recovered from being axed for giggling after the Worthington Cup exit at Bristol. Perhaps it was the behaviour of today's youth or simply the misdemeanours of millionaire teenagers. In my day, a timely clip round the ear would have saved his career.

Gordon Watson

Pedigree

Umea
IFK Gothenburg
AC Milan
Parma
Manchester United
Everton
Charlton Athletic

Born: 1974
Tavelsjo, Sweden

Blue Stats

	apps	goals
League	10/5	1
FA Cup	2/1	0
Other	0	0
Total	12/6	1
2001/02		

If Jesper Blomqvist could have steered clear of injury, he'd have been priceless. How can you not be impressed by his courage in overcoming a terrible injury? Goodison Park had become the place where players go to hide or die - but not for Blomqvist. He was a player with something to prove and the early signs were encouraging. He gave us extra width as well as an injection of class. With every club in the Premiership searching for a winger possessing his portfolio of skills, it was disappointing to see him move on.

Jimmy Husband

Danny Cadamarteri burst onto the Merseyside scene like a whirling dervish at the same time as Terry Owen's lad but their careers have taken different paths. The dreadlocked kid was thrown into a very poor side but endeared himself to Everton fans with a blinding goal against the Reds. Unfortunately, his electric pace couldn't make up for his immaturity and lack of composure. He was never given time to hone his technique in the Reserves and soon lost his swagger. After grabbing headlines for a late-night assault, he slinked through the exit door at age 21.

Alan Whittle

Pedigree

Arsenal
Leyton Orient (loan)
Leicester City (loan)
Nottingham Forest
Trabzonspor
Everton (loan)
Everton

Born: 1970
London

No matter what the future holds, Kevin Campbell has been a Number 9 worthy of the famous shirt. After all, he almost single-handedly lifted us away from the drop-zone in 1999. Kevin has finished top scorer during his first three seasons and was rewarded with a handsome five-year contract - which was quite a bonus for a 30 year-old. Although the big man has had bad luck with injuries and has lost a yard of pace, he's retained his human touch. 'King Kev' is one Premiership star who never refuses to sign autographs. He's an absolute gentleman to boot.

Dave Hickson

Pedigree

Derby County
Blackburn Rovers
Coventry City
Everton

Born: 1974
Birmingham

Despite giving us the thumbs down during Howard Kendall's third spell, Lee Carsley was signed by Walter Smith to halt the downward spiral in our fortunes. The Gravesen-lookalike is rugged and pugnacious - the type who would start a fight in an empty room - and has brought much needed steel to midfield. I must add that some of his challenges are as subtle as a brick in the face. All the same, his hell-for-leather approach invariably allows him to come away with the ball. Admittedly, Carsley has won few plaudits for creativity but could be a useful building block.

Wally Fielding

Mr Carter is the Will Cuff of the post-war era. He joined the board back in 1975 and, despite wild fluctuations in our fortunes, has been there ever since. I'd argue that he brought unparalleled success to the club whereas a minority would counter that he's also overseen the decline of the Merseyside Millionaires. In my eyes, he's had a becalming influence during the bad times when squads have resembled something to be returned to Littlewoods after Christmas - a mix of rash purchases and unwanted gifts. He's a toff for whom I've always had the uppermost respect.

Gordon Watson

Pedigree
Everton
Blackpool (loan)
Born: 1982
Southport

Peter Clarke is an uncompromising player. He was schooled at Bellefield by Dave Watson - and it shows. He's a chip off the old block. I get the impression that, given the chance, Clarke would run through a brick wall for Everton, rebuild it and run through it again. He'll need to polish up his passing skills but it's definitely time for the teenager to have an extended run at centre-back. I believe in Joe Mercer's faithful maxim: *"If he's good enough then he's old enough."* Youngsters like Hibbert, Chadwick and Clarke need to be patient and grab their chance to shine.

Brian Labone

What can I say about a towering striker who rarely scores? Duncan Ferguson has got so much ability and, when focused, he's unbeatable in the air. But scoring goals is his job and he doesn't do that too often. Despite a catalogue of injuries, disciplinary problems and a prison term, 'Big Dunc' became a cult-hero who inspired an FA Cup triumph during his first spell. Then he was sensationally sold to Newcastle only to be bought back at a knockdown price. Unfortunately, his Goodison love affair has soured. Perhaps, half-fit talismen have no place in the Premiership.

Fred Pickering

Pedigree

Newcastle United
Tottenham Hotspur
Lazio
Rangers
Middlesbrough
Everton
Burnley

Born: 1967
Gateshead

Blue Stats

	apps	goals
League	18/14	1
FA Cup	3/1	0
Other	1/1	0
Total	22/16	1
2001/02-01/02		

Paul Gascoigne is a national treasure. He's the finest footballer of his generation and the best attacking play-maker that I've ever seen. 'Gazza' won the hearts of the nation in Italia 90 and no Scotsman will ever forget his goal in Euro 96. Although his tabloid life always over-shadowed his playing career, he worked hard on regaining his fitness during his Goodison swan-song. 'Gazza' played as if every game was his last and inspired his team-mates with the joy that he brought to the park. Players like him come along once every 50 years.

Alex Young

Scot Gemmill helped revitalise a seemingly doomed squad in the fight against the forces of gravity but never received the praise that his tireless efforts deserved. Perhaps the fans have been too eager to compare him with Archie Gemmill. His technique isn't as good as his dad's but he's inherited a Rolls Royce engine which enables him to glide from box-to-box. In recent panto seasons, he's rolled up his sleeves and conceded nothing until arithmetic dictates that he must. Nowadays, the Gemmill name is synonymous with perspiration rather than inspiration.

Wally Fielding

Pedigree

Oldham Athletic
Everton
Oxford United (loan)

**Born: 1973
Heywood**

Goalkeeping can be a thankless job - ask Paul Gerrard who has weathered a hurricane of criticism over the past six years. Keepers are isolated for most of the match with only their confidence for company - and sadly that precious commodity has deserted him on occasions. He's a good keeper who has been capped at Under-21 level by England but, after winning an uphill fight to secure his place from Thomas Myhre, suffered lapses in concentration which led to several soft goals. His best years may still lie ahead but are unlikely to be at Goodison.

Jimmy O'Neill

Blue Stats

	apps	goals
League	2/3	0
FA Cup	2	0
Other	0	0
Total	4/3	0
2001/02		

Caveat emptor! Evertonians welcomed David Ginola like art lovers gazing at the Mona Lisa. But frustratingly, the 1999 Footballer of the Year had misplaced his smile and managed only one or two flashes of flair before many Goodison connoisseurs concluded that he had joined the herd of toothless white elephants grazing round the watering hole located in Liverpool 4. No doubt, Ginola will be remembered as one of the lost treasures of the Everton dug-out. It was one of Walter Smith's last rolls of the dice and a lavish gamble destined to end in ignominy.

Alex Young

Blue Stats

	apps	goals
League	38	1
FA Cup	3/1	0
Other	0	0
Total	41/1	1

1999/2000-00/01

When fit, Richard Gough had a stabilising influence on those around him. The veteran member of the Ibrox clan had won every honour north of the border and was lured to Goodison by Walter Smith as a stop-gap measure. His initial form was a sensation but his susceptibility to injury diluted his overall impact. Possibly, his decision to stay for a second term may have stalled the progress of younger talent and some critics even considered him a wrinkled pantomime dame who refused to leave the stage. On the contrary, I regret that he hadn't joined us 15 years earlier.

Gordon Watson

Pedigree

Vejle
Hansa Rostock
Hamburg
Everton

Born: 1976
Vejle, Denmark

Thomas Gravesen arrived with the nickname 'Mad Dog', however I've often wondered what breed the Hamburg fans had in mind when they gave him that title. He's impressed me with his attacking surges but tackling does not appear to figure prominently in the terms of his remit. Gravesen's technique is top notch but his discipline isn't and he has been red-carded for silly transgressions. While Walter Smith vowed the Dane would never play for Everton again, I just hope that his new boss can get him to harmonise the forces of yin and yang in midfield.

Wally Fielding

Thomas Gravesen

Pedigree
Everton
Arsenal
Born: 1981
Liverpool

Blue Stats

	apps	goals
League	37/12	18
FA Cup	6/1	1
Other	1/2	0
Total	44/15	19
1997/98-2000/01		

Franny Jeffers was a boyhood Blue, who unlike Robbie Fowler and Steve McManaman, pledged his future to his first love. I've seen hundreds of hot prospects in my time but there is something special about Jeffers. His stick-like appearance only serves to hide his skill and courage but I'm most impressed by his astute movement off the ball. Possibly too frail to fulfil his potential on the larger international stage, our future lies at the feet of youngsters like him. His loss would be the loudest of the death knells that have tolled mournfully at Goodison in recent years.

Gordon Watson

Pedigree

Elfsborg
Stabaek
Everton

Born: 1979
Marseille, France

Walter Smith was at the end of his tether when he snapped up Tobias Linderoth while the fans were caught up in the whirlwind hoo-ha associated with David Ginola. Linderoth has been given little opportunity to acclimatise to life in the Premiership but, even when he has played, he's lacked the presence to make everyone dance to his tune. So much so, it took Blues by surprise when he whistled one over the England crossbar in the 2002 World Cup. He looked a decent centre-circle anchor for Sweden. Whereas at Everton, we still don't know what to make of him.

Wally Fielding

Pedigree

Nuremburg
New England Revolution
Everton

Born: 1971
Irvine, USA

Celebrated as a soccer superstar on the other side of the Atlantic, Joe-Max Moore appeared to adapt effortlessly to the all-action mayhem of the English game. His alertness and clinical finishing allowed him to poach six goals in his first 11 matches before his shine began to dull. While he's never been short of courage, he's often come off second best against the more physical opponents. Moore has seen far less action over the past season but I still think that it beggars belief that he has been awarded 100 more caps than some Blue legends - like me!

Sandy Brown

I've known every Everton manager - every one of them. I like the look of David Moyes and trust that the fans show patience while he steers us into the top-half of the table and then on into Europe. He's already collared the slackers and I've few doubts that everyone knows where they stand with him. Of course, Moyes will be judged on his ability to extract the best out of the men available to him. Hopefully he can combine the fitness of Ian Buchan, the horse-trading of Harry Catterick with the team-spirit of Howard Kendall and avoid the luck of Gordon Lee.

Wally Fielding

Mr David Moyes

Pedigree
Whitehill Welfare
Heart of Midlothian
Everton
Born: 1978
Edinburgh

Good signings always seem blindingly obvious - with the benefit of hindsight. Gary Naysmith was recruited to beef up Walter Smith's squad and has been an unqualified success. In particular, I like the way that he hurries and scurries up and down the touchline. In an era of expensive Ferraris and Porsches with limited warranties, Naysmith represents a durable Land Rover. Well, that was until last winter. The wing-back had become so dependable that, with Everton on life-support, his untimely break-down could have pulled the plug on our plans.

Alex Young

Pedigree

Luton Town
Derby County
Sheffield Wednesday
Benfica
Everton

Born: 1970
Merthyr Tydfil

For one reason or another, the Goodison jury is still out on Mark Pembridge. Personally, I give him the thumbs-up. While he doesn't possess the finesse or flair to have got many games in any of Harry Catterick's teams, I must admit that I've been impressed by his old fashioned work ethic. On matchdays, there isn't anything sophisticated about his frenetic approach. Pembridge simply zips around the middle of the park like a blue-arsed fly closing down and harassing opponents. I liken him to a dodgem - he has limited control and is often involved in collisions.

Sandy Brown

Pedigree
Tranmere Rovers
Everton
Born: 1979
South Shields

I'm not sure how it happened but Steve Simonsen arrived at Goodison as the most expensive keeper in the Premiership. Not only did nobody know who he was but it took him about three years to get a game. Capped at youth and under-21 levels by England, he has the potential to follow in the giant footsteps of Neville Southall. Whereas, a big fee can hang around the neck of a young star for years gradually choking confidence, Simonsen has exhibited many of the exuberances of youth. I'd say that he's made the Number 13 jersey his own - for now.

Gordon West

Aided and abetted by Archie Knox, his sergeant-major, Walter Smith did more deals than any Goodison boss. With a healthy kitty, he introduced international stars like Dacourt and Materazzi. When the cash ran out, he was forced to trawl through the bargain basement as well throw kids like Ball, Dunne and Jeffers into the deep end. Towards the end his tactics were dour, the entertainment was nil and the relegation trap-door beckoned. Walter Smith was a good man betrayed by people on and off the pitch. He was no stranger to success - at Ibrox.

Alex Young

Pedigree

Bolton Wanderers
Celtic
Everton

Born: 1971
Kirkby

Alan Stubbs is one of us. He was released by the club as a youngster but has overcome much bigger set-backs having battled testicular cancer on two occasions. As a free transfer from Celtic, he's been a terrific addition. At first I feared that he'd be vulnerable to the Premiership's speed merchants but his initial form has been rock solid. It's obvious that his commitment to the royal blue cause is in his blood and, if he can put in a few more seasons of quality defending, will be a worthy addition to Gwladys Street's Hall of Fame.

Brian Labone

Pedigree

Athletico Paranaense
Liaoning Bodao
Everton (loan)

Born: 1977
Liaoning, China

Goodison's array of exotic talent must be a spelling test for the Megastore staff. Their task has been exacerbated by the arrival of Li Tie and Li Wei Feng as part of the sponsorship deal with Keijan. A solid defensive midfielder, Li Tie was signed to build his own great wall in front of our often exposed rearguard. But he's turned out to be more than a barrier. He can pass and shoot, too and certainly isn't out of his depth in the Premiership. The newcomer also enjoys superstar status in Beijing which will no doubt make EFC a household brand throughout Asia.

Brian Labone

Pedigree
Everton
West Ham United
Aston Villa
Everton
Born: 1973
Chorley

David Unsworth was a boy-wonder during his early days and matured into a key member of the 1995 FA Cup-winning side. I remember the fabulous job he did in shackling Mark Hughes in front of the twin towers. More recently, he's been reinvented as the burliest wing-back in the Premiership. 'Rhino' has received stick from the punters for his pre-occuppation with seeking Duncan Ferguson's head from 50 yards. Whereas from 12 yards, he's almost as accurate as Roy Vernon. But certainly no-one can find fault with his major asset - his enormous heart.

Brian Harris

Pedigree

Newcastle United
Aston Villa
Everton

Born: 1974
North Shields

I've a lot in common with Steve Watson and recommend that he concentrates on what he does best - defending. I was also a full-back who was propelled up-front in an emergency - only to be criticised for my lack of goal-scoring expertise. I looked sharp in training but the mayhem on matchdays was a different kettle of fish. Like Watson, I also committed the sin of scoring an own goal or two. The fans forget game-saving tackles and goal-line clearances but always remember own-goals. Watson should heed my advice, it makes going to the pub much easier.

Sandy Brown

Pedigree

Celtic BC
Falkirk
Heart of Midlothian
Everton

Born: 1970
Falkirk

Davie Weir is a dedicated professional who'd be my first name on my team-sheet for Everton and for Scotland. The central defender has never failed to impress me with his near-faultless displays and was Walter Smith's best buy. I'd go as far to say that he's usually unflappable on the ground and often majestic in the air, occasionally defying gravity. Of course, Weir has had his work cut out with everyone around him playing out-of-position but he's taken it all in his stride. I also detect that he wears his shirt with a pride that is noticeably lacking these days.

Tommy Jones

Will he be Mr Wright in name only, or can David Moyes' key capture in the close-season finally fill the chasm left between the goalposts ever since the legend that was 'Big Nev' hung up his gloves? Richard Wright can take heart from Southall's early experiences - dropped following a traumatic Goodison derby and farmed out to Port Vale to hone his temperament. Wright has the raw material - witness a stunning penalty save at the Stadium of Light. But he'll have to work on his powers of concentration to gain the confidence of the Everton fans and England manager.

Alan Whittle

Pedigree

Marseille
Standard Liege
Everton

Born: 1980
Kono, Nigeria

Joseph Yobo faced Michael Owen and Gabriel Batistuta during the World Cup - and walked away with his reputation substantially enhanced. But Evertonians have learned the hard way that international tournaments and the rough and tumble of the Premiership are very different arenas - witness Daniel Amokachi. In one respect Yobo has proved himself a natural at Everton. He picked up an injury within minutes of his first appearance in a friendly! But when he finally made his Premiership debut, it was with all the poise and pace he had showed in Japan.

Brian Labone

Right Back   *Right Half*   *Right Wing*   *Wright Plonker*

Gone But Not Forgiven

Evil spirits continue to undermine our ambitions and, if luck really is earned on the training ground, I propose that we re-locate the Gary Speed Gates to Bellefield and decorate them with heads of those who have sinned against us. All managers have had a sinner or two in their midst. Harvey's dabbles overseas realised Atteveld and Rehn. Still those two fared better than Royle's continental misfits - Thomsen and Hottiger. Whereas Bilic and Williamson were fall-out from Peter Johnson's friendship with West Ham. In fact, my bronze spike candidate arrived from Upton Park. David Burrows was a hapless defender whose dodgy pedigree fuelled a legion of conspiracy theories about Reds in the boardroom. Mike Walker deserves the silver spike for guiding us to the brink. The gold spike sinner? It has to be Brett Angell - a dinosaur representing the dark world of fallen standards.

Mark Tallentire

Walter Smith signed Ibrahima Bakayoko from Montpellier for £4 million - surely it was a case of mistaken identity. Perhaps he never adjusted to the hustle of the Premiership or was homesick for the Ivory Coast. Whatever the reason, Bakayoko was an unmitigated flop. I realised that his days were numbered when his team-mates confessed that they had no idea what he was going to do most of the time. I took this to mean that they thought that he was rubbish. His career was mirrored not by his sensational free-kick at Bristol but by his fluffed penalty against Sunderland in the Worthington Cup. I remember that Goodison held its collective breath as Bakayoko was called up to take part in the shoot-out. His woeful effort was delayed by the farcical sight of the referee insisting that the striker remove his track-suit before taking the spot-kick.

Mark O'Brien

Geary, Latta, Johnson, McNamara, Hickson, Xavier and another dozen players have made the controversial switch across Stanley Park. Many were better players than Nick Barmby, most were better loved. So why did the inoffensive Humbersider's move cause such a furore? Was it his so public pronouncements of affection for Everton only months previously? Was it that the Everton fans had rejoiced when his rediscovered form earned him an England recall after four seasons of under-achievement? Or was it his revelation that as a boyhood Red he had dreamed of playing in front of the Kop? Whatever the reasons, the Everton fans felt utterly and hopelessly betrayed when Barmby elected to follow the path with no redemption. They await his return to Goodison, albeit now swathed in the colours of Leeds United, with baited breath.

Mike Hughes

All of the truly great managers have made mistakes in the transfer market but jaws dropped when Harry Catterick traded young David Johnson to Ipswich for Rod Belfitt in November 1972. The so-called sharp-shooter arrived from Portman Road cutting a pop star figure. But his Beatle mop failed to conceal the fact that he fired blanks - one after another. Predictably, his alliance with the Goodison faithful was to prove unholy and fruitless and he was never destined to join the tradition of great Everton Number 9s. The non-scoring striker struggled in all of his 20 outings alongside a succession of partners including the hapless Joe Harper and the volatile Bernie Wright and managed just three goals. As for young David Johnson - Evertonians cringed as he went on to represent England and accumulate domestic and European honours with our red neighbours.

Chris Gill

Rod Belfitt

There is no shortage of candidates for a rogues' gallery. Some were rash purchases, others were simply promoted beyond their abilities. One woeful striker, who failed a trial under Howard Kendall but was considered good enough by Mike Walker, achieved success elsewhere. Ditto an unhappy Swede who returned home to being voted Player of the Year. And what about the erratic African? I suppose it depends how much weight is given to his FA Cup semi-final cameo. Even Harry Catterick signed a pub footballer after a cup tie. Then there was the centre-half who disappeared during a derby match never to be seen again. And, of course, the lesser-spotted Barmby. Who gets my thumbs down? It has to be Alan Biley who resembled Rod Stewart in looks and technique. He was bought in haste and tolerated for longer than is good for the soul.

Len Capeling

On the fiftieth anniversary of the 6-0 defeat at Hillsborough which sentenced us to three years in Division Two, a new society was launched at a fantasy football gala to honour the men who had made unique contributions to our decline. The top-table sparkled with guiding lights such as Messrs Finch, Marsh and Walker - who cradled the famous poisoned chalice - and grown men wept as Angell, Bakayoko, Biley et al marched into the strains of Gerry and the Pacemakers. Perhaps the biggest ovation was reserved for the guest of honour, Mr Johnson. Predictably, not everything went to plan. The tables had been decorated with red cloths and the menus had been printed upside down. Still these minor set-backs didn't dampen the mood. The attendees were comforted by the knowledge that every single penny would benefit one of Everton's ex-players. Slaven Bilic, take a bow.

Mark Staniford

Peter Johnson was chairman of Everton Football Club Company Limited between 1994-1999. The less said the better!

Gordon Watson

Thomas Myhre was a showboater who loved to be loved. I first saw him in a Pontin's League game at Ewood Park when he was on trial from Viking Stavanger. His performance was a cocktail of spilled shots and flapped crosses and I encouraged my friend, an avid autograph hunter, to get his signature after the game because we were unlikely to see him again. Inexplicably, the club paid £800,000 for his signature and Myhre showed his appreciation seven months later by almost dropping us into the Nationwide. Leading Coventry by the skin of our teeth, the news flashed that our relegation rivals were trailing at Stamford Bridge. Goodison took a deep breath of relief - that was until Myhre fluffed a modest header from Dion Dublin and we had to endure 10 minutes of nerve-jangling hell. At the final whistle, he had the nauseating gall to applaud the fans.

Steven Milne

Tommy Myhre

Appearances can be deceptive. Stephen Price wore blue and white and looked like a football fan, whereas Alex Nyarko wore blue and white and looked like a player. Their worlds collided on a miserable afternoon at Highbury where we were being totally out-classed. Nyarko was simply going through the motions when Price staged a one-man pitch invasion to remonstrate with him. He merely vented the frustrations of the thousands of travelling Blues and offered to change places with the player in the belief that anyone could have showed more commitment, especially at £1 million per year. Obviously, his spontaneous act of madness cannot be condoned. The fan was banned from watching football, his fine being paid from whip-rounds in local pubs. The player received a more severe sentence. He was exposed as not being fit to wear the shirt.

Ian MacDonald

Alex Nyarko

Ask anyone who ever met him and you'll hear the same story - Mike Walker was a likable man. But no matter how much you might have liked him - he liked himself more. The Everton boss constructed an image of vanity among those who worked around him during his 11 months at the helm. There was a suggestion - never proved - that the snow white follicles were artificially enhanced. But the deep tan was natural and worked on at every opportunity. On the pre-season tour of Sweden, he would conduct press conferences on the hotel balcony and insist that I sat with my back to the sun so he could catch more rays. Later in the day he would spread-eagle himself by the pool, resplendent in an orange thong, while his players sniggered. The self-styled silver fox started the new season with a run of four draws and 10 defeats and was sacked.

Vic Gibson

The writing was on the wall courtesy of a ringing endorsement from a colleague. The reporter had predicted: *"Bakayoko is the new George Weah"* and in similar vein proclaimed: *"Williamson is a midfield maestro with rare skills."* In reality, Danny Williamson produced one solid performance in 17 games. During his three seasons, he was consistent in keeping his skills under wraps and in demonstrating an embarrassing sensitivity to criticism. *"Speed continues to work unceasingly, while Williamson continues to under-achieve,"* I wrote at the nadir of his career. Stung by such a vitriolic attack Williamson made obscene gestures towards me with his right hand, while waving the offending article in the other. He did so from the team-coach idling outside Elland Road, with half an inch of reinforced glass between us. A week later, he was gone. I sometimes wonder what happened to the Cockney funster ... but not for too long.

David Prentice

Bernie Wright was a shot-putt champion and a member of the England Under-19 rugby union squad but never mastered the round ball. He first cast his monster shadow in our direction in an FA Cup tie. Although the Walsall striker was ill-equipped for the big-time, Tommy Casey, our caretaker-boss while Harry Catterick was in hospital, saw something in young Frankenstein that had escaped everyone else. He was immediately anointed 'Bernie The Bolt' by Gwladys Street. Was it a sarcastic reference to 'The Golden Shot' television show or more do with the fastening device through his neck? Either way, he was out of his depth. I thought that he was the innocent victim of circumstances. That was until April 1972 when Bernie Wright was allowed to wear the famous Number 9 shirt. It was a sight for sore eyes and he should've known better!

George Orr

I was in Starbucks with the founder of Gwladys Street's Hall of Fame when all heads turned as Richard Gough and Abel Xavier strode in. I'd interviewed them on many occasions and offered them copies of my friend's latest book. As they relaxed, I could see them engrossed in reading about the history of EFC and could hear them talking about the accomplishments of Dean, Mercer, Young, as well as a few characters sporting walrus moustaches. After half-an-hour they returned to our table. They were both genuinely excited. The Scotland star enquired: *'If I hang around Goodison long enough do you think I'll get into the Hall of Fame?'* The author hesitated and surveyed the two giant defenders towering above him. He looked them both up and down and responded: *'You may well do Goughie but your mate has got no effing chance!'*

Garry Doolan